EDITH A. JENKINS

AGAINST A FIELD SINISTER

memoirs and stories

CITY LIGHTS BOOKS

SAN FRANCISCO

Cover Design: John Miller/Big Fish Books

Library of Congress Cataloging-in-Publication Data
Jenkins, Edith A.
   Against a field sinister : memoirs and stories / by Edith Jenkins
      p. cm.
   ISBN 0-87286-263-1 $7.95
   I. Title
PS3560.E4833A7   1991   813' .54—dc20

91-21313 CIP

City Lights Books are available to bookstores through our primary distributor: Subterranean Company. P.O. Box 168, 265 S. 5th St., Monroe, OR 97456, 503-847-5274. Toll-free orders 800-274-7826. FAX 503-847-6018. Our books are also available through library jobbers and regional distributors. For personal orders and catalogs, please write to City Lights Books, 261 Columbus Avenue, San Francisco CA 94133.

CITY LIGHTS BOOKS are edited by Lawrence Ferlinghetti and Nancy J. Peters and published at the City Lights Bookstore, 261 Columbus Avenue, San Francisco, CA 94133.

The following have been published in:

Feminist Studies, Vol. 7, No. 1, Spring 1981
  "With Stones from the Gorge"

Massachusetts Review, XXIII, No. 3, Autumn 1982
  "Against a Field Sinister"

Room, A Women's Literary Journal, No. 7, 1982
  "In the Wings of the Jump"

The Threepenny Review, Fall, 1989, Vol. 10, No. 3
  "The Following Wind"

This book consists of a selective record of a life from approximately 1917 to 1991.

Three of the pieces — "Stretto," "The Ineluctable Silence of the Lake," and "Distances" — seemed to insist for the most part on the conventional chronology and form of the short story. Because the tale in each case is not primarily that of the narrator, I have permitted myself the storyteller's right to telescope and elide. Taken as a group, and somewhat to my surprise, these seemed to make a statement on the perceived choices of gifted and intellectual women of that period and the tragic consequences thereof. However, to summarize in this way reduces experience to ideology in a manner that the stories do not.

The other memoirs are as scrupulously accurate as memory will allow with but a few very minor changes to protect the living. In these, although I have not courted discontinuity, I have given the "shaping spirit" full rein in the knowledge that underlying and prevailing themes may provide a continuity more real in recording a life than does simple chronological order. And such wayward form seems appropriate in recording a woman's life wherein there is so characteristically a refusal to separate the personal and the political, in which the private and the outside world reflect what Donne would call an interinanimation of each other.

E.A.J.

TABLE OF CONTENTS

STRETTO

When Franz and I were about to be married, Catherine's mother sent a wedding present and with it a letter. The present was a set of light yellow place mats and napkins with firm white embroidery in wreathlike patterns. I still have the doilies, but I use them infrequently because the napkins were somehow thrown away in a spate of mindless spring cleaning. I had not heard from Catherine for a long time. On the familiar, gray stationery with the insignia Menlo Park House engraved on the top of the page, the letter explainecwhy. "During one of her brief periods of lucidity," it read, "I told Catherine of your impending marriage. She was so pleased and asked me to send you a present from her. . . . Most of the time she does not seem unhappy but just very far away."

The last time I saw Catherine, she had just returned from the East, where she had been studying music. I was in the early part of my second year in college, luxuriating in the heady atmosphere of English classes with Mr. Ruth, basking in his praise of my work.

Catherine's mother had called for me at my parents' house in San Francisco. In her large, chauffeured limousine with the separate cab for the driver, we chatted now with greater ease than we had when I was a girl, though I was still awed by her decorous speech and took its decorum for a kind of privileged wisdom. As we drove toward Menlo Park she entertained me with an anecdote. I do not remember the content, but I remember the humor was enhanced by the solemnity of her presentation. "You know," I observed, "you tell stories exactly the way Mr. Ruth does."

Catherine and I were delighted to see each other. She was recuperating from a taxi accident she had been in during the previous winter in New York. It was in the days before antibiotics, and when osteomyelitis had set in, she was in excruciating and prolonged pain. Despite her suffering, she was even more remarkably beautiful than she had been earlier, her Botticelli hair haloing her face, but her beauty seemed to pause on the threshold of womanhood, to be still that of a girl — austere, asexual.

•

"You look," said Catherine's sister, "like Joan of Arc seeing a vision." We were sitting in the library, and her sister was looking at a photograph. It was fall. I had just turned fifteen and had come down from San Francisco to visit Catherine for the weekend. Although I had known her parents were rich, I was not prepared for the size and grandness of their estate. The rangy house sat at the end of a long, winding driveway that found its way through an orchard of plum trees. The smell of warm plums hung in the autumn air. The house itself was surrounded by lawn, and the lawn was bordered with flower beds. The main floor of the house consisted of a large, conventional dining room, kitchen and pantry, a living room and a library, and a separate bedroom for each parent. In the picture Catherine sat in almost full profile, her mouth slightly open, her diaphanous hair forming a crown of light around her face, her expression rapt, peaceful, distant. Her sister's remark: the common polarities — the smart girl and the beautiful one. Some invidiousness, perhaps. Perhaps some prescience.

At the dinner table Catherine's mother presided. I remember thinking her hair and skin were a kind of desert monotone, but behind the monotone of the skin was the suggestion of youthful freckles. I noticed how before she spoke her mouth gathered itself as if at attention. And the nicety of her words, how sparingly and with what regard she employed them. "Children," she adjured in response to an exchange between the younger sister and the brother, "if this recrimination continues, I shall be forced to ask you to leave the table." I was awed by the restrained and lofty language of reproof. The recrimination ceased.

While Catherine practiced piano the next morning I wandered into the library and leafed through a copy of *The Atlantic Monthly* I found resting on the coffee table. In it I found two poems by Catherine's mother, one called "Reprieve" and one, untitled, beginning with the line "Do not bid me walk among your graves." Catherine's mother surprised me as I finished reading. Embarrassed, I told her that I liked the poems, and she, addressing me as if I were an adult, asked me what contemporary poets I read. We discussed Elinor Wylie and Robinson Jeffers, and then we talked about Emily Dickinson.

After we finished chatting, I joined Catherine in the living room and listened as she went over and over a phrase in a Bach two-part invention. On the top of the grand piano I noticed a picture of an elderly man. Catherine, I suppose observing me looking at it, stopped. "That," she told me, "is Carl Jung." She said her parents had spent long periods in analysis with him, commuting between Menlo Park and Zurich. Laughing, although somewhat sadly, I thought, she continued, "Three years ago my mother came back from Switzerland a 'thinking introvert' and my father, a 'sensation extrovert.' Last summer my mother returned an 'intuitive extrovert' and my father, a 'feeling introvert.' " We joked about grownups, how women our mothers' age interested themselves in psychology, wore peasant blouses, and took up folk dancing. Composing a parody of a folk dance full of jocundity and the pseudo-pastoral, we performed it for ourselves with mock expressionless faces.

In the afternoon we stopped by a lawn chair where Catherine's father reclined under a walnut tree. He was reviewing, he said, a brief in a case concerning the rights of the Navajos. He seemed remote in the way of fathers, but I felt his remoteness was composed of other elements as well.

There is a memory I have that will not subject itself to the scrutiny of other recollections. It involves Bertha. Catherine said she had been their nurse when they were younger. Her present function was not clear. Sometimes she carried freshly ironed linens in her arms, but there always seemed to be the smell of warm linen about her. Periodically throughout the day she attended to tasks in the children's bedrooms. During these times Catherine and her sister, and to a lesser extent the boy, seemed to be drawn into contact with her, and when they were, their movements seemed fluid and easy, whereas downstairs they moved in a discrete and angular manner.

On Sunday evening after dinner Catherine and I walked through the orchard. Because it had not yet rained, the earth was a light, soft tan. In the piebald dusk we stepped on soft clods of dirt under the trees. I told Catherine about my high school — the gray asphalt yard, the girls' locker room with the high smell of sweat. I talked about the camp where we had met that summer, and quoted Emily Dickinson: "I never felt at Home — Below — / And in the Handsome Skies / I shall not feel at Home — I know — / I don't like Paradise —." Catherine said, "When I think of camp, I smell the small tornadoes of dust rising with every step we took from our tent to the redwood dining table. I see the dust on my boots. I feel it on my skin. I remember the gritty feel of dust on my teeth." And as the sky darkens over the orchard we both suddenly recall the tall nights in the Sierra, the quiet collusion of the trees, and the cold, fiery corridor of the shooting stars.

•

I was fourteen the summer we met at Huntington Lake Camp for Girls. It was the first girls' camp in the West, and I suppose that was the reason such strict rules were imposed. Each girl had a health chart with six questions to be checked off every evening:

Did you brush your teeth morning and evening?
Did you eat all your vegetables?
Did you have a bowel movement?
Did you take part in setting-up exercises?
Did you go out for two of the following activities?

a) swimming
b) hiking
c) horseback riding
d) nature study
e) crafts

I placed a check after each of the above. But then there was the troublesome one:

Did you drink six glasses of water?

At home I never drank water. I did not like it, and I did not seem to need it except on a hike when I was hot and my mouth got dry. Each day I forgot until bedtime, until it was time to fill out the health chart. If the chart was not perfect, our tent could not win a citation in the morning no matter how carefully we had swept the dusty wooden floor with a wet broom, smoothed down our lumpy sleeping bags on the metal springs of the cots, raked the pine needles from the bare earth beneath them. For seven days I forgot and let down my tent mates. Then I adopted a nightly routine. Taking my tin cup to the faucet, I filled it and drank it down. The cup measured one and a half glasses. Four times I filled it and drank it down. A check on the health chart. The metallic taste of the cup in my mouth. My stomach gurgling like the partially filled hot water bottle I got at home for a stomach ache. In the middle of the night I had to take my flashlight through the pungent, scary, pine-dark night, fifty yards to the outhouse. No one awake but me. The outhouse smelling of wet wood, wet toilet paper, excrement. When I crept back into bed, the sleeping bag felt cold, impersonal, dank in the tree-laden dark, a dark punctuated by stars and the strange, anonymous animal sounds.

On hikes we climbed up steep trails where the altitude left me breathless and thirsty. It was important to be a good sport, jolly and uncomplaining like the blonde society girls from Piedmont and counselors with names like Pinkie and Mitch. You were not a good sport if you asked to stop and catch your breath or if you stopped to drink water from a cold Sierra stream. If you drank water when you were hot, you might blow up and founder like a horse. I could picture myself with a swollen belly, lying on my side, unable to turn. We hiked past banks of flowers — Indian paintbrush, wild iris, and the translucent purple-blue lupine, poisonous to horse and cattle. If we took a test on the names of flowers, trees, and birds, we could get credit for "Nature Study." My sock was crawling into my boot, and I felt a blister forming. The boot had six holes and six hooks that had to be laced. You were not a good sport if you stopped to fix your sock.

Once a week there was a ceremony at nightfall in a clearing between the trees in what the camp administration had named Honor Grove. All the campers sat on the ground in a large semicircle while the counselors marched in two's, each one carrying a candle, and stopped when they reached the center of the space. Here two girls would be named Honor Girls. By vote of the counselors, they had been selected for their sportsmanship. Miss Grace, the camp director, and Miss Dean, the head counselor, handed each girl a scroll. When the two girls were named, there was an outcry; there was hugging and kissing and there were tears.

Almost every girl had a crush on an older girl or on a counselor. The counselors had crushes on older girls or on each other. Miss Grace had a crush on Miss Dean this year, whereas last year, I was told, she had favored Miss Brown and chosen her as head counselor. The first week of camp, as my tent mates and I were passing the makeshift office Miss Grace shared as living quarters with Miss Dean, we had seen Miss Brown and Miss Dean wrestling furiously on the dusty ground before the door, Miss Dean's impeccable pink tweed knickers and matching blouse covered with swirls of dust.

Soon after our arrival in camp I had made a new friend. I had noticed both Catherine and her sister as the girls gathered at the bus stop to embark from San Francisco, standing apart from the others, thoughtful, self-contained. Catherine was a year younger than I, very beautiful, her yellow hair translucent around her face. I think our bond was that we both felt like outsiders. The second week we tried to organize the girls to protest the award and point system which dominated every activity. "Why can't we simply enjoy the riding and swimming and crafts just for themselves?" our delegation asked Miss Grace.

In our leisure time Catherine taught me songs unlike the ones we sang around the campfire each night. Sitting on the shores of the lake with our bare feet dangling in its waters, we sang "Full fathom five, thy father lies," and taking turns as the captain and the chorus, we laughed as we acted out the captain's song from *Pinafore*.

•

The same year that Catherine went East to study music, I went to college in Berkeley. My parents had arranged for me to board at the home of a professor of Italian and his artist wife. The Carsons' modern redwood house was situated in the Berkeley hills where the back windows looked across the bay to San Francisco, and the front, across the street to a steep, wild meadow. Mr. Carson was a very short man with what appeared to be almost a noble head—high brow, white hair, luminous and responsive eyes. The smell of Irish tweed seemed always to announce him as he entered a room, walking in his crepe-soled shoes, with his weight upon his heels and his body cast forward at an angle to compensate. Merry and communicative, wearing his prodigious learning lightly, he was in sharp contrast to his wife. Camilla Carson was tall, upright, serious and somehow fugitive. Giving the impression of beauty without being beautiful, she wore her auburn hair cropped short and close to her head. In conversation she tipped her head slightly to one side in a pose associated with listening. She adorned herself with Navajo jewelry, earrings, necklace, belt, carved silver studded with turquoise. It was the time of the "rediscovery" of the Indians. Mrs. Carson attended soirées where Tony Lujan, Mable Dodge's husband, sang Indian corn and fertility songs. On those occasions she wore a homespun cape and slung the left front panel over her shoulder so that the Navajo belt hanging loosely at her hips revealed its turquoise studding. Always she seemed remote and vague, as if responsible to some absent overriding authority.

The lofty two-story living room of the Carsons' house, accommodating library, piano, and phonograph, was decorated with large surrealist and cubist paintings. One with great orange and brown forms was painted by Mrs. Carson. In the evenings after dinner Mrs. Carson retired to her room. It was then that the professor introduced me to his treasured record collection. Night after night he invited me to share with him the exaltation of the music. Playing the Haydn Clock Symphony, he told me to listen to the ticking of the clock and to the runs that seem both to yield to and to defy it. He introduced me to Brahms' first Piano Concerto. "Listen to that Rubinstein go!" he chuckled.

On the grand piano at the far side of the room there rested a framed picture of a now familiar visage, and on the photograph, an inscription, "To my dear friend, Camilla Carson, Affectionately Carl Jung." One night as we sat on the piano bench looking through record albums, Mr. Carson nodded ruefully in the direction of the picture. "My wife," he said, "spent three summers studying with him. There are a bevy of them," he sighed. "Babe Ruth, among others in the English Department, is one. They have all been to him, and they all scrape and save to go the long hejira to Zurich as often as they can. They meet, along with the parents of your friend Catherine," he said parenthetically, "in what is for them the arid spaces in between."

The professor's room was a balcony above the living room. He described it, laughing, as Juliet's balcony. My room, at the front of the house on the second floor, looked out wide windows at the greenness of the wild grass on the hillside across the way. Adjoining my room was Mrs. Carson's. On her bureau, in a tarnished brass frame supported by two brass legs spraddling out behind, was a picture of Catherine's father. In it he stood jauntily in front of an old Studebaker, a cap on his head, a large-bowled pipe in his hand. Over Mrs. Carson's bed on the wall a Navajo rug was hung.

•

The following year I moved into my own apartment on La Loma, just below a stable that rented horses to students in the university's riding classes. I had not decided definitely on a major, but I registered for two courses given by Mr. Ruth, Survey of English Literature and an individual study course in creative writing. Familiarly known as "the Babe," a soubriquet I heard he enjoyed, Mr. Ruth was a small, slight man. He wore wire-rimmed glasses with pink protectors where they gripped his nose. He had large, rather buck teeth, and the struggle to keep his lips closed over them made him appear as if he were perpetually trying to suppress a laugh, an appearance that was not totally misleading. He was pre-eminently the academic—cloistered, cerebral, unathletic, one in whom the body itself seemed a kind of addendum. But his lectures were interlarded with hilarious tales of confrontation between town and gown, in which he, as David in academic attire, slew with his arrow of wit a ruddy Goliath of a truck driver usually referred to as "the bruiser."

Through friends in graduate school I had access to the giddy and bawdy gossip of the English Department. The Babe was a bachelor, I heard, and spent long summer afternoons sitting naked around the men's pool in Strawberry Canyon, a satyr Socrates in lotus position, exhibiting, as if unknowingly, a cock of gigantic proportions, and rocking with mirth over some recondite, ribald tale he recounted to an admiring circle of students.

During my second semester in Survey of English Lit I fell in love. In retrospect, it is hard to believe how I felt my stomach drop, my breathing arrest when I saw his Grecian profile, his shock of blond hair, his sensual mouth. A reader for Mr. Ruth's class, he did not seem even to notice me when he returned the papers in the passageway in Wheeler Hall. Shamelessly, I followed him, found where his classes were, where he ate, what concerts he attended. When I finally screwed up my courage to speak to him, the occasion was a penciled note, one I did not understand, on my blue book. I met him in Mr. Ruth's office where he conferred with students by appointment. After the conference he asked me to join him for a cup of coffee. I thought I noticed Mr. Ruth eyeing us as we left. A few days later, Bruce asked me out for a date. I think he was dismayed by my intensity and, perhaps, by my innocence, for I did not see him again.

Late in the spring semester I went by Mr. Ruth's office to pick up a series of love or, more exactly, lovelorn sonnets about Bruce that I had submitted to Mr. Ruth for the directed writing course. Although he had annotated the pages with unqualified words of praise (curiously, I now think, for the work, though skilled, was highly derivative), I noticed a distinct chill in what had been his heretofore jovial reception. "Have you seen Bruce?" he asked as I left the office, and as I replied that I had not, "If you do see him, tell him that I am looking for him." I hoped he did not know that Bruce was the subject of my sonnets.

The weekend before finals I skipped my customary visit to my family. On Sunday evening, quite unannounced, Mr. Carson knocked on my door. "Would you like to have a walk," he asked, "or are you committed relentlessly to being a grind?" Flattered by his attention and receiving his teasing as permission to leave my books, I walked with him up La Loma to where there was no longer a paved road, up the steep hill, past the stable to where we could look down upon the flatlands and the San Francisco skyline across the bay. I think he was feeling some responsibility to my parents, and he hummed and hawed in embarrassment before he introduced the subject which I subsequently surmised was the occasion for the walk. "I met that young blade," he joked, no doubt in order to cover up his discomfort, "who reads for Mr. Ruth. He told me that Mr. Ruth said you were writing fine love sonnets," and he paused a moment, "to a woman." I could feel the color rising to my face. I did not know whether I was more taken aback at the lie itself or that Bruce, the unknowing subject of the poems, should be the recipient and purveyor of the misinformation. "But," I heard myself stammer, "those sonnets were about Bruce, Mr. Carson, and they were clearly written about a man. Why would Mr. Ruth make up such a tale?"

I did not see Bruce again until my senior year in college. I was then way past the romantic pursuit of unrequited love. "Hey, Bruce," I called to him one morning as I saw him in the Co-op, "how about a cup of coffee?" He joined me at the counter, and we chatted easily about what had transpired since last we had seen each other. When I asked him about the Babe, he said, "I don't see much of him anymore. You know," he continued, "he's been in love for years with a married woman and she with him, but she is afraid to leave her husband for fear of triggering some instability in her kids. Apparently her family has a devastating history of mental illness. Anyway, he seemed increasingly cross with me, so I've been avoiding him."

•

When Franz and I were married, we rented a small flat in Berkeley. Franz was tall and dark, with black winged brows, and moved with the confidence of one who had grown up working in wheat field and lumber camp. We had met my last year in college when Franz went to work as a

14

teaching assistant for Mr. Carson and accompanied him one Friday evening to a party for Loyalist Spain.

Franz and I had become increasingly involved with protest movements. We marched against unemployment. We organized support for the lumber strikes up north. We raised money for the communist paper. Consequently, when Mr. Carson called Franz into his office to tell him that because of cuts in the university budget he would not be able to keep him on, we were not disconcerted. Now, we thought, Franz would go back to being a worker, and the working class would be the catalyst of social change in a dying social order.

Jobs, however, were hard to find. Briefly, Franz had work in a fish processing plant and came home each night with the smell of fish in his clothes, in his hair, in his hands. Then all the new workers were laid off. Because it was the middle of the Depression and because I had a B.A., I qualified for a job as social worker with the State Relief Administration. Seasonal workers from the canneries and fields of southern Alameda County and fired factory workers lined the waiting room in Hayward. My assignment was to determine whether fmilies I interviewed were eligible for relief. Uneasy in the role and inept in filling out the long forms, I once made a mistake, and a family could not get food for two weeks. In the evenings when I arrived home, although Franz had dinner ready, he was distracted and detached. An ineffable sadness had settled on our marriage, but I did not want to face it.

We were not sad, however, when on Friday nights we met our friends from the university at a local night club. Gathering in the back room we dubbed Cafe Society, we drank and sang and discussed the world and our lives. Our friends too were all active in the Left—either on the campus, organizing teaching assistants for better wages, supporting the peace movement, raising money for Loyalist Spain, or in the SRA in the union that had just been formed of state, county, and municipal Workers. We sang Brecht-Eisler songs like "Come out fields and workshop! / Rise up workers, farmers." Or perhaps Franz sang a cowboy song of his Oregon youth, "Left my girl in the mountains, / Left her standing in the rain. / Went down to the station. / Caught myself a southbound train."

That year in an article in the *Berkeley Gazette*, I read of Catherine's father's death. After mention of his survivors, his professional affiliations, the notice stated that the family requested donations be made to a fund for the Navajo Indians. In response to my letter of condolence, Catherine's mother wrote me. She said, "Catherine is in a private sanitarium in New Hampshire. She has her own cottage. She is well attended."

One evening in the course of our attempts to raise money for Loyalist Spain, Franz and I paid a call on Mr. Ruth. He had never met Franz before and he was his most outgoing and generous. When he found Franz was unemployed, he seemed to sense his feeling of unworthiness, and he went to great pains to put him at ease, drawing him out about his origins and early life. Franz talked about the long hours of work during the wheat harvesting in the Northwest, about working stripped to the waist, about strength and camaraderie and endurance. Mr. Ruth's admiration showed in the intensity with which he kept his lips taut and closed over his teeth, the concentration with which he watched Franz's every expression. Franz grew expansive. He told him about his uncle who was an organizer for the Wobblies, about how he had been arrested during the Butte, Montana, copper strike in the twenties, how he had spoken to him about class struggle and how workers throughout the world were faced with the same enemy. His uncle seemed very real to me. Mr. Ruth, that night, seemed a bystander, outside the sweep of history, learned, effete.

Shortly thereafter I saw a note in the vital statistics of the newspaper that Mr. Ruth and Catherine's mother had been married. I phoned and asked if I could visit them. Ensconced in an old and elegant house on the ridge of Berkeley that overlooks the gentle Contra Costa hills, Mr. Ruth was splendid in his part of the old bachelor newly married, and Catherine's mother was as ever warm and articulate and dignified. Franz did not accompany me on this visit.

One night Franz did not come home. I did not hear from him for ten days. Then in a letter postmarked Los Angeles he asked me to meet him there at the Hotel Driscoll. When I arrived, there was no trace of Franz. As evening came I felt as if I were being pulled by gravity into a terrible hollowness within my stomach. I remember looking down at the courtyard from my room on the tenth floor and feeling a different gravity, and I was afraid. Over and over in my head I heard the aria "I know that my redeemer liveth," and though the words bore no reference for me, they seemed somehow a prophecy of doom. The next morning Franz arrived, but we could not speak.

•

I had moved to San Francisco alone. For six months I had been working in a department store as main floor cashier, standing in a cage behind a bulletproof window. Working people coming to pay their bills around the first and fifteenth of each month pushed money or checks through a trough under the window. I retrieved the payment, punched a receipt on the cash register, slipped it back to the customer.

One Wednesday evening as I returned home from a shop stewards' meeting I saw a familiar gray envelope in the mailbox. I read the letter as I mounted the steep stairs of my North Beach apartment. On the restrained stationery under the identifying place name, Menlo Park House, the letter proceeded: "Dear One," it said, "Your note awaited me on my return from a brief trip East to visit Catherine after Mr. Ruth's death last month. Thank you for your sweet words. He had been suffering greatly in the last weeks. I have had to attempt to regard his death as release." The letter continued, "Catherine is physically well but remains very much within herself. Bertha stays with her these days and reports that she does communicate with her, though not in words. At times she plays her piano, which I had sent to her cottage." And then, a stanza of a poem I had submitted to Mr. Ruth during my sophomore year. I had not looked at it since. It read: "Mingle with sorrow nothing. / It is best pure. / It is best like a single shaft of light. / Thus it will not endure." "How," she wrote, "did you know so much about grief when you were so young?"

On the days between the fourth of the month and the fifteenth and between the eighteenth and the end of the month, work was slow. Saleswomen across the aisle exchanged complaints about their men. A child fingered some merchandise. The store detective loitered, bored, looked up when he heard the percussion of my cash register.

In the slowness of time I hear the percussion of the clock in the Haydn symphony. The high ceiling of the store becomes a vaulting living room in the Berkeley hills. In my ears, the Handel aria "I know that my redeemer liveth." Traceries of Zurich in the drawing rooms of Berkeley and Menlo Park. Catherine, her pale halo of hair. Traceries of white on the pale yellow doilies. Mr. Ruth in the canyon, bawdy, ebullient. The long line of unemployed and the meticulous denying forms. Franz's large presence in the small flat. Bystanders. The live, small personal despair and no redeemer. The huge despair of Spain. I do not want to be a bystander. (I slip a receipt through the trough beneath the window.) I want to be part of the cleansing wave that will change the world.

AGAINST A FIELD SINISTER

In the Florence flood as the waters rose higher and higher, we fled first to the third, then to the fourth, and finally to the sixth floor, where the rooms were no longer luxurious but were little and bare like the rooms in a boarding house, and we did not know whether the Albergo Berchielli would float down the Arno with us in it or whether we would go flailing out the windows to join the flotsam of tables and car tops and showcases and manikins with their pink legs in the air making V shapes as they sped down the immense clamor of the river. The smell of benzine filled the hall where the hotel guests gathered to take a census in case we did not all survive, to parcel out some stale bread that had been kept for the dogs, and to ration the few bottles of mineral water and Coca-Cola that were available. My sister Ethel was there with her husband Jacob; my aunt with my Uncle Jeff, who was eighty and had never been out of the United States before; my husband Dave and I, and Rachel, our youngest, who had paused in her travels to join our family reunion. When evening came and there were no lights, Rachel and Dave and I moved two beds together, kept our clothes on and snuggled all night to protect ourselves from the cold and to protect Rachel from the shakes.

It is strange about fear. My uncle was afraid that night because for all his life he had been a sheep rancher and the enclosing frightened him. Dave was afraid, my sister said, because he is used to human situations over which he can exert some control and he could not control the flood. And Ethel, because she was sick with anemia, bone-weary and overdue for a liver shot. Nevertheless, she said "If only some of us can escape, it's clear it should be all the young people." Madie, my aunt, kept her usual calm, and Jacob did a crossword puzzle and we never knew how he felt. I am in no way a courageous person, but I do not seem to panic when there are no alternatives. Like before an operation that I know I must have. Or when I was a girl jumping horses, once I was in the wings of the jump and there was no way out. In those thirty hours we were never confronted with choice, though we might have been had the flood not subsided by morning. But it did, and we made our way across a plank above the slush to the washed-out street overlooking the bedraggled Arno.

Half of Florence was still inaccessible with water and mud deep on the streets, washing against the Ghiberti doors of of the Baptistery, invading the Santa Croce Museum, encircling the American Express building. Everyone we passed had the same vacant, shocked look. People greeted each other shaking their heads in disbelief and murmuring, "Disastro, disastro."

We struggled onto the train for Milan, seven of us fighting up the steps through the solid body of refugees, ourselves muddy, disheveled, exhilarated with fatigue and relief, but each occupied with a private drama of what might have been.

•

Vineyards patterning the steep hills of Tuscany, the dusky olive orchards, the medieval castles: "Landscape," I thought, "plotted and pieced — fold, fallow and plough," and looking at the working men on the train, "And áll trádes, their gear and tackle and trim." The centuries-old beauty of the countryside untouched by the marauding waters.

•

I still have the book of Hopkins I neglected to give back to Jean. It is on my shelf, filed between Herrick and Housman. Contrary to my normal, disorderly habits, I have all the poetry in alphabetical order by the authors' names. Whenever I take down the *Poems of Gerard Manley Hopkins*, I look first at the name Jean Tatlock inscribed on the flyleaf and under it the date, April 1938.

It was long after Jean took her own life that I found the sonnet "No worst there is none. Pitched past pitch of grief." With poems like Hopkins', I can read only a few at a time, and I go back to those few very often, and thus it is that even with a slim volume such as his, it may take me a lifetime to read it all. I discovered the poem one winter when I had done some cliff-hanging of my own, and it was only later that I thought of the lines in relation to Jean: "O the mind, mind has mountains; cliffs of fall / Frightful, sheer, no-man-fathomed. Hold them cheap / May who ne'er hung there . . . ."

•

Jean was very private about her despair. She had always been close about her life and her decisions, so that although I was surprised when she told me as a fait accompli that she was registered in medical school, I felt the decision came from some place in her that I never had presumed I knew. When I saw her after her first year, she had already decided to become a psychiatrist. The schoolwork seemed easy for her. Each summer she returned from the East, and each summer we resumed our friendship.

She was private, too, about her relation with Oppie. All of us were a bit envious. I for one had admired him from a distance. His precocity and brilliance already legend, he walked his jerky walk, feet turned out, a Jewish Pan with his blue eyes and his wild Einstein hair. And when we came to know him at the parties for Loyalist Spain, we knew how those eyes would hold one's own, how he would listen as few others listen and punctuate his attentiveness with "Yes! Yes! Yes!" and how when he was deep in thought he would pace so that all the young physicist-apostles who surrounded him walked the same jerky, pronated walk and punctuated their listening with "Yes! Yes! Yes!"

And somehow one always knew he felt guilty about his gifts, about his inherited wealth, about the distance that separated him from others. Jean said, "You must remember that he was lecturing to learned societies when he was seven, that he never had a childhood, and so he is different from the rest of us."

•

I read recently that when the atom bomb was dropped on Hiroshima, Oppenheimer said, "Now we have known sin." I had until then considered sententiousness a reasonably innocent, if annoying, fault. After I saw his statement, I remembered an evening at John and Mary Ellen Washburn's, a party to raise money for Loyalist Spain. The house on Shasta Road had become a kind of salon for those who desired respite from the halls of academe—professors, graduate students, the Berkeley intellectual Left. Mary Ellen, tall and commanding, presided over the gatherings, her hearty laugh turning always into paroxysms of asthmatic coughing. I see her in a narrow, full-length batik dress and above it the long, columnar neck, the short wiry hair, black against her white face, and the inviting warm smile so that in her presence one felt like a small state suddenly granted diplomatic recognition by a major power.

Oppie rented the flat below, where the house was built on stilts into the steep hillside, and frequently found his way to their living room for social events. On this occasion, he had just delivered himself of an epigram. His admirers stood about in the awe-inspired response his pronouncements evoked when John Washburn, older than Mary Ellen and much older than the rest of us, deep in his cups and in the solitary wisdom they allowed him, mumbled, "Never since the Greek tragedies has there been heard the unrelieved pomposity of a Robert Oppenheimer." With that, he laid his head upon the table, a Tenniel dormouse, fast asleep.

I have thought since how the notion of tragedy, with all its exceptionalism, all its tawdry grandiloquence, even then attached itself to Oppie.

•

Jean and I discovered the metaphysicals about the same time. "Whoever goes to shroud me, do not harm / Nor question much / That subtle wreath of hair, which crowns my arm; / The mystery, the sign you must not touch. . . ." Jean was enamored of Donne, and I, of some of the lesser poets. "Throw away thy rod / Throw away thy wrath / Oh my God / Take the gentle path . . ." wrote Herbert. It has always been something of a wonder to me that I who am not religious find myself so much attracted to both religious poetry and music, but I think I detected already then, as I have since, that I translate religious devotion and its mood of elevation to a humanist equivalent. Einstein once described a religious person as someone who is attached to superpersonal values, and I read to my surprise that old Handel, himself, was a man of the Enlightenment and at most an agnostic when he wrote *The Messiah*.

When I became totally immersed in the Movement, I stopped reading poetry or listening to religious music because I could not rationalize my preferences with Party edict. I am not sure Jean was ever so doctrinaire, though we shared the same political beliefs. I remember the pleasure with which I discovered a poem of Emily Dickinson's that conformed with the Marxist aesthetic: "Unto like Story — Trouble has enticed me — / How Kinsmen fell — / Brothers and Sister — who preferred the glory — / And their young will / Bent to the Scaffold, or in Dungeons — chanted — . . . Feet, small as mine — have marched in Revolution / Firm to the Drum — / Hands — not so stout — hoisted them — in witness — / When Speech went numb . . . ."

Jean introduced Oppenheimer to the poetry of John Donne. When the trial bomb went off in the Jornado del Muerto in New Mexico, Oppie dubbed it "Trinity" after Donne's sonnet "Batter my heart, three-personed

God . . . ." That was approximately six months after Jean's death.

•

Two events in which I found myself involved in the spring of 1935: at the University of California in Berkeley, a meeting to protest the expulsion of a communist student was broken up by the football team with the full support of the coach; at San Mateo Junior College the following day, a meeting to which UC students had been asked to speak turned into a violent riot, with the dean standing by and the cops escorting the visiting students firmly across the bridge.

Only one member of the faculty at Berkeley gave shelter and moral support to the trailed and terrorized students, a professor of French, Haakon Chevalier.

•

In 1937, Alfred Stern left Germany accompanied by his mother, Hedwig Oppenheimer Stern, his wife, Lotte, and their two children. He had refused to arrange for his own departure until he secured exit visas for many other Jews. Upon arrival in the United States, he, like all the other refugee doctors, was required to repeat an internship and to pass the State Boards. Oppie was very helpful to the Stern family during that period.

After he had delivered my second child in 1945, Dr. Stern was approached by the FBI and questioned about me. He did not know precisely what they were searching for, he said, but they asked if he knew my first name. He laughed his shy laugh as he recounted the exchange. He was in the habit, he told them, of knowing the first names of women whom he delivered. Apparently, he did not co-operate to their satisfaction, and his application for citizenship was held up.

•

Jean and Hazel and I took a week off in the summer and drove up the Mendocino coast. Hazel was already seeing Aubrey, and Jean was in one of her off periods of the many on-and-off sequences with Oppie. Jean had a roadster, and the top was down. We were all elated with the salt air and the beauty of the countryside.

Jean had a fine contralto voice, and we sang our way up Highway 1. I taught her "The Silver Swan" and told her how, when the English Singers performed, they recited the lyrics first so that the spoken words remained in one's ear and formed a counterpoint with the many voices of the madrigal. " 'The silver swan,' " I said, trying to reproduce the diction of the English Singers, " 'who living had no note,' and in your mind you have the spoken voice that does not sustain the word 'living' the way the singer must, 'When death approached, unlocked her silent throat, / Leaning her breast against the reedy shore, / Thus sung her first and last, and sung no more. / Fárewell, all joys,' and then," I said, "the alto comes up underneath singing, 'Farewell, all joys; O death, come close mine eyes; / More geese than swans now live, more fools than wise.' " And Jean taught me a song from *Twelfth Night*. " 'She never told her love,' " she sang as we wound up the narrow road, and Hazel, who did not sing, listened in appreciation. " 'she never told her love, / But let concealment, like a worm in the bud, / Feed on her damask cheek.' "

I had not connected this song consciously with Jean's death, but years later, when I was first able to write about her suicide, the lyric forced its way into the poem. And that other one she taught me as well, the one in which Dido, surrounded by her handmaidens, sings from the funeral pyre she has herself erected: "When I am laid in earth, / May my wrongs create / No trouble in thy breast. / When I am laid in earth, / May my wrongs create / No trouble in thy breast. / Remember me! Remember me! / But ah, forget my fate."

•

I cannot place the time exactly, but it must have been around the period of the 1937 Moscow trials. Oppie said he came to me because he knew I would not be shaken in my political loyalties, and he needed to talk. He had just heard from the Austrian physicist Victor Weisskopf of the arrest of Soviet physicists. He was reluctant to believe the report, but he could not dismiss it. I think word of those arrests sowed the seeds of his disillusionment with the USSR and, eventually, the American Left. He was depressed and agitated, and I suppose now I know how he was feeling, but then I was scornful of what I saw as his gullibility. Curiously, try as I may, I cannot recall where this interview took place, although I think I recall every word that Oppie spoke.

•

When Jean came home from medical school during vacations, she sometimes spent a few days at the Washburns'.

The summer of her mother's dying, Jean grieved for her and burned with rage against her father, who, out of his own need and weakness, would not let her die. And Jean seemed to need Mary Ellen. I see Jean's tall frame as she stands by the Washburns' fireplace, how straight she was except for the large breasts. I think of her blue eyes and their heavy lashes, and the one eyelid that, from some childhood injury, always drooped. Then I remember Mary Ellen describing their friendship, how I was puzzled at the time by a kind of aside. She said, "When I first met Jean, I was put off by her breasts and her thick ankles."

The Washburns' house was made of redwood and was approached by wooden steps descending from the road, steps shaded and almost concealed by eucalyptus, pine, and acacia. You could not see the house itself until you were almost upon it. As Mary Ellen opened the door, the heavy smell of acacia was joined by the smell of her cigarettes, the high medicinal smell of Life Buoy soap, and then the tart wool smell of the Indian rugs. The room you entered was completely dominated by the fireplace, and somehow everyone gravitated to the madras-covered double mattress that served as couch. Behind the living room, separated from it by a narrow hall, were two bedrooms and, between them, a bathroom. Mary Ellen and John slept in separate rooms, a not uncommon practice at that time. I surmised the arrangement afforded Mary Ellen escape from John's fairly persistent drinking. So that when I clambered up the hill from my apartment on Tamalpais Road below, to have coffee with Jean and Mary Ellen on a Saturday morning, I thought nothing of the few occasions I let myself in the unlocked door and found them sitting up and smoking over the newspaper in Mary Ellen's double bed.

•

During the war, I was working in Hale's Department Store as main-floor cashier. There were two windows in the bulletproof cage where Beulah and I shared a shift. When Dave was scheduled to return to the Pacific theater in the merchant marine, I wanted to be sure to have his child in case he did not come back. Since we did not know how much time he would have ashore and we did not want to be delayed by the three-day wartime waiting period in California, we took off a week and went to Nevada to get married. On the way over the Sierra, we were snowed in at Donner Pass and spent the night at a hotel. In the morning I broke out with chicken pox, but we went on to Reno, and Dave bought me a slim, silver Navajo ring with four turquoise stones as a wedding band. We found a judge who married us in less than five minutes. Although we thought we did not want a real ceremony, we felt angry and dishonored by his dispatch. Dave said, "Here's five dollars," and he said, "Ten, please," and I thought, "I hope he gets my chicken pox." We stayed in a motel for five days while I was pretty sick. Dave bought food and cooked for us, and later we figured Margy was conceived the night of the blizzard at Donner Pass. When I was a little better, we drove to Pyramid Lake and sat in the car and talked about our lives together when the war was over and about the struggle for a better world.

•

No one told you in those days how your labor was progressing. After sixteen hours, when a contraction came, I thought I was caught forever in a prison of pain. I yelled at Dave, "Never again!" and he said, "Think of the women having babies in Stalingrad now." I wanted to scream at him for his rebuke and for his part in causing a pain he could not share, but it hurt too badly. Then they wheeled me into delivery, put my feet in stirrups and gave me some stirrups to pull on with my hands. I remember these were asymmetrical and therefore hard to pull, but I could not say anything. Soon Alfred Stern told me how to use the pains, and it felt better. Shortly after, I gave a big push, and there was a slithering that felt like a fish, and they said, "It's a girl!" and I called Dave and shouted, "Dave it's a girl! It's a girl!" The next morning they brought her to me. She was pink and beautiful past belief, with the apertures of her nostrils curved like tiny leaves, and we named her Margaret for the actress who played Miriamne in *Winterset* and Ludmilla after the woman sniper, Ludmilla Pavlichenko, who killed 180 Nazis during the siege of Stalingrad.

•

Jean stayed with us for about a week in our San Francisco apartment on Buena Vista East. She enjoyed holding Margy, and on the particular day I remember, she stood with the baby in her arms, looking out the window at the green park across the way. Dave had not yet come home, and we were having the kind of intimate discussion we had not often had in the days when we were really more intimate. Oppie was already married to Kitty. I asked Jean if she regretted refusing to marry him, and she said, yes, she did not think she would have done so had she not been so mixed up. I recall responding perhaps it was that she perceived him as essentially nonsexual. Jean put her cheek against Margy's and held gently the baby hand that was pulling her hair and said, "Maybe you're right. I wish I could meet a man like Dave."

For all the confidential exchange, I felt somehow remote from her, however. I thought it was the fact that she was now a Freudian analyst and we considered Freud and Marx unreconcilable, though she claimed she was still a Marxist. But I did not feel close, and when her suicide note appeared in the paper, I could not grieve. I thought perhaps it was that I knew she wanted to die. And besides, her note did not let us mourn, because it said, "To those who loved and helped me" (not "who tried to help me" — how considerately she chose her words even then) "all love and courage . . . ."

•

"Some people, I think, were motivated by curiosity, and rightly so; and some by a sense of adventure, and rightly so . . . ." — from Robert Oppenheimer's "Speech to the Association of Los Alamos Scientists," commenting on motives of scientists who worked on the bomb, November 2, 1945.

". . . from a technical point of view, [the bomb] was a sweet and lovely and beautiful job." — from Oppenheimer's testimony before the Personnel Security Board of the U.S. Atomic Energy commission, April-May 1954.

"Thou hast abused the glorious gift of thine understanding!" — from the first German *Faust*, quoted by Erich Heller in the essay, "Faust's Damnation; The Morality of Knowledge," 1959.

"[Faust] acquire[d] a virtuosity inappropriately superior to his virtue." — *ibid.*, Erich Heller commenting on Goethe's conception of Faust.

•

If one lives long enough, one has a catalogue of one's own historic guilt, and though it is presumptuous to think the individual suffering conscience a matter of any consequence, those like me who did not apprehend the full horror of the bomb at the time, lulled by our need to see the end of what we knew to be a just war, feel a measure of complicity.

I read in *Hiroshima Diary* how the survivors examined themselves day and night for petechiae, the ruby blisters, knowing in two weeks after the redness appeared they would be dead. As I think about them, I hear Marlowe's line: "See where Christ's blood streams in the firmament."

•

When I first heard of Oppenheimer's testimony on Bernard Peters, I could not believe it. Yet the messenger, whom I do not even now feel free to name, was one who had loved Oppie very dearly, had belonged to the little group of devout apostles at the University of California, and had followed him from Berkeley to Los Alamos. He sat in our living room, hunched forward in his chair, his brow creased with pain as he insisted Oppie was utterly changed from the man we had once known.

It was shortly after the close of the Korean War. McCarthyism was in its heyday. In our discussion of that war, he

seemed uneasy with us in what he termed our "Left ortho-
doxy," but not nearly so disapproving as he was of Oppie.
We had not seen our visitor since early in 1944. He was at
that time apparently assigned to some work in Chicago,
where we had a night's stopover on our way to visit Dave's
family in New York. We had asked him to meet us. He came
to the hotel, and we walked to a restaurant together. I remember his hands shook as he held the menu, and when
Dave asked him about his research, he said he was not free
to discuss it. I asked whether it concerned the German
speculations on splitting the atom, a matter he had mentioned in Berkeley some years before the war. Visibly shak-
en, he replied, "You have much too good a memory."

Now world War II was long over, the bombs long since
dropped on Hiroshima and Nagasaki. We had heard little
of Oppie since that time, and we asked eagerly about him.
He told us Oppie had testified before a secret session of
the House Un-American Activities Committee in 1949, and
his testimony had been leaked to the *Rochester Union
Times*. Asked to comment on his friend and former colleague Bernard Peters, Oppenheimer had said Peters
could not be trusted because he had escaped a German
concentration camp through guile.

•

School mornings I got up at a quarter to seven, squeezed
oranges, made French toast or scrambled eggs and called,
"Breakfast ready in three minutes!" Becky was ironing her
skirt in the kitchen, and I would say, "Can't you do that
anywhere else? You're right in my way." Margy and Rachel
needed their hair braided, and Davy was going to be late if

he could not get the tangles out of his shoelaces. Then they were all gone. I went back to bed, but it did not feel good. Sometimes I woke up about eleven and did not know what I wanted to do or should do. I would feel a panic rising, rising in my throat. One day when I was downtown, the panic rose until I almost did not know where I was; so I took an N car uptown and dropped in to see Hazel and Aubrey, and I felt a little better, but only for the moment.

Shortly after, the Krushchev report hit the press. Although the Soviet-haters were not surprised, we who had linked years of humanist struggle to our belief in the USSR were shocked past understanding. We swung between anger at those who had deceived us and at ourselves for our own part in our deception. For had not the data been available to our unwilling eyes? The first year I retreated into the mood of private despair my private crisis had foreshadowed. And I knew the personal crisis had, itself, reflected doubts I had refused to entertain — those ritual Sundays of leafleting and doorbell pushing, those endless meetings with the formulae gone dry.

Someone said to me, "The mark of the democratic personality as against the totalitarian is its ability to tolerate ambiguity."

•

It was not a good winter for us when we got back to London after the Florence flood, though we knew it was a luxury being there on my sabbatical, and our children were grown and on their own in the United States, except for Rachel, who was now hitchhiking in North Africa, and I was committed only to immerse myself in British theater. But

London rained unceasingly so that the rain seemed in a continuum with the flood, and the gray Thames, an ancient, ponderous reminder. Each morning we left our flat on Baker Street and walked to the underground with the dismal stalls of W. H. Smith at the entrance or wandered through Regents Park, and it seemed as if every morning led to the turbid questions of the night in Florence with the noisy Arno spilling over the walls onto Lungarno Acciaoli and charging past the clogged Ponte Vecchio and the random men and women in the hotel, stunned into the intimacy of the flood. And in each of our minds: who would be saved if it had come to that? We had seen *Measure for Measure* in Edinburgh that summer, and I thought how Shakespeare knew that fanciful solutions or chance ones, such as our escape from the flood unharmed, left the dark questions still unanswered: as when one wakes, heart pounding from the grim triage of a dream, glad it was all a dream, but shaken by the specter of its choices. What would have been our choices? How does one measure in the scale the weight of lives? Dave argued for those one loved and for one's own life. I argued my sister's stand, to save those who still were young. And I hated Dave for his pragmatism as he hated me for my untried mock heroics.

We went to see Olivier in *Othello* at the National Theatre and saw in the program notes how he trained his voice until he could speak an octave lower that his natural pitch, and we saw the Living Theatre production of *The Silence of Lee Harvey Oswald*, and we saw Paul Scofield in *The Staircase*, and a seldom produced play of Brecht's, *The Life and Death of Arturo Ui*, in which Chicago gangsters are presented as Hitler, himself, and the play becomes a study of power and complicity with evil, and at The Fortune we saw

36

In the Matter of J. Robert Oppenheimer, a play based loosely upon the transcripts of the hearings before the Personnel Security Board of the Atomic Energy Commission.
During the intermission, we heard groups of people discussing Jean and Oppie and how Lieutenant Colonel Lansdale had them watched the night they spent together
subsequent to Oppie's marriage, and in the play, when
Lansdale was asked why Oppie had spent the night with a
former lover who was also a Communist, he had replied,
"If you had loved a woman who had been a Communist
and she was in deep trouble and she wanted to see you, I
hope you would have gone, too." And Dave and I felt as if
we were eavesdropping at our own funeral.

•

The first year after my sister's death, I felt to go on was
the breaking of a covenant. My nephew called to tell me,
and the news passed through me the way a knife passes
through your hand, cleanly, so at first you feel no pain.
When the pain, the unremitting pain, began, I kept thinking, and all through the services at the cemetery and after I
came home I kept thinking of death as "the beggar's nurse
and Caesar's" and how when that fabled woman put the asp
to her breast, she became gentle and resolute. I felt my sister was within me, but it did not lessen the pain. For my sister did not take her life, and although she was ready for
death, she did not want to die. Later, I understood for the
first time what the poet meant when he wrote: "After the
first death, there is no other."
We had become close again after the long self-righteous
years were behind me. She had forgiven me, I think, for
them, and I did not ask her to understand that I still envi-

sioned a different world nor did I tell her of what I was ashamed and of what I was still proud.

•

I saw Alfred Stern in his office shortly after Oppenheimer appeared before the AEC Personnel Security Board, where his Left background was being revived to pillory him eight years after the termination of World War II and upon the occasion of his opposing further research on the H-Bomb.

In the course of the Security Commission Hearings, they reviewed Oppenheimer's bizarre and contradictory testimony to various agencies and security officers. Alfred and I had both read for the first time how Oppenheimer, in the early years of the War, named his closest friend, Haakon Chevalier, as the contact in an attempt to secure information for the Soviet Union. We had read how subsequently he dubbed the whole elaborate tale a cock-and-bull story. We read how now, confronted with both accusation and denial and asked for explanation, he responded in an apparent agony of self-deprecation, "Because I was an idiot!" We saw also in the news how he had spoken of Jean Tatlock, so many years dead, of her politics and of her love for him.

Alfred Stern shook his head. I saw the clear Oppenheimer eyes squint with pain. "I can only think of it as a kind of breakdown," he said.

•

Historians who write about Oppenheimer like to speak of him as tragic hero downed, depending on their predi-

38

lections, by, first, *hubris* in his insistence on the dropping of the Bomb or, second, weakness in character in tangling himself in a network of lies.

For a time I saw him as protagonist in a drama of the grotesque, elevated to high station for his invention of a demonic weapon and brought down by his subsequent opposition to an even more demonic one. Now I think of him divested of all such heroic fictions which serve in life and literature to obscure acts themselves in all their minute and vast and particular human consequences.

●

Jean was discovered by her father. The door of the Telegraph Hill apartment was bolted so that J. S. P. Tatlock, who was old then and Emeritus Professor of Chaucer at Berkeley, climbed through a window and found her. She had taken a lot of sleeping pills and was lying in the bathtub. I cannot get the picture out of my mind how her large breasts must have floated in the water. He had no right to see her that way. Her note had said: "all love and courage." She had not in any way abandoned hope except, that is, for herself.

●

In the spring of 1980, Haakon picked us up at the Hotel de L'Abbaye. I should have expected him to look old, but I was somehow surprised, and I was touched by his frailty. His wife and companion in exile had died a year and a half before, and he had for company a gentle poodle called Quinette. We went to a restaurant, Chez Maître Paul, near

L'Odeon, one that he had heard recommended — he did not eat out often — and we talked about the past and made friends with the couple at the next table, who were celebrating their first anniversary. They insisted on buying us each a brandy, and we all promised to meet there in two years. Soon Haakon turned the conversation to Oppie. We felt him still struggling with his love and confusion and dismay, and he said he thought of Oppie as a tragic hero. I found I could not tell him how I did not want to think in those terms anymore. He said it was safe for him to return to the United States now, and he might do so. On the way home to the hotel, as we passed the Saint-Sulpice, I had an attack of *turista*, and Dave and Haakon, who were both lame, ran with me back to the restaurant. Then Haakon drove us to our lodgings, and we said, "We'll phone you tomorrow to say goodbye."

WITH STONES FROM
THE GORGE

"I hate it in a net, " she said, "how it flattens the bun until you might as well have it short."

"When I don't wear one," I told her, "the messy strands flail out from the middle of it."

In the *San Francisco Chronicle* the reporter called it a *chignon.* I had said, "I have spent my entire adult life working for peace, and you call me before the committee for advocating force and violence." The reporter wrote, "Shaking her *chignon* in emphasis, she said, 'If peace means force and violence, I am for force and violence.' "

That was the time I had asked Letha to take care of my children if I went to jail. For months afterwards, I jumped whenever the doorbell rang. Davy had nightmares. He said the Brahms "Sandman" was a scary song to sing to children at bedtime.

•

In the summer I cut my hair. It had always been long except for the year I was twelve when my aunt took me to have my curls cut off and I looked mournful and unattractive and wore a white middy blouse with a blue serge collar and a pleated blue serge skirt. We didn't have to. I just wanted to. Ernie and I wore high laced shoes so the other girls would know we were too young for high school and must be smart.

My hair was dark brown. You could tell it wasn't black by the orange glints it had in the sunlight. My cousin teased me. He had made up a name for me and called me "black-haired Ephus." That made me mad. Not because I disliked black hair but because it wasn't true. Like a teacher saying, "I never think if I'm teaching boys or girls," and you knew she was lying. Anyway it was an all-girls school. I had crushes on two of the teachers. When Miss O'Brien went by with her blond hair piled on top of her head and her clear Irish skin, I felt a wet swelling between my legs. I worried a lot about being whatever you called a girl fairy.

The gray halls of that school. The damp sweat smell in the basement gym. You brought a note from your mother once a month. It said, "Please excuse my daughter from physical education for three days as she is unwell." I thought the school was like a low forehead, like a low ceiling where you'd bump your head if you stood up. Only the maiden-lady teachers and the rules: The verb "to be" does not take an object. The word "like," when used to introduce a comparison, is a preposition and is followed by the objective case.

•

The next year, I discovered Emily Dickinson. During study period, I wrote over and over in my binder, "To make Routine a Stimulus / Remember it can cease — / Capacity to Terminate / Is a Specific Grace —." Sara Bard Field read Emily Dickinson's poems at four different bookstores. I went to all the readings. Sara Bard Field's hair had turned white, I was told, when her son was killed in a car she was driving. Every poem she read I coded with a small *o* in the table of contents of my copy and on the page where the poem appeared as well.

Sara Bard Field had been married, and her preacher husband would not give her a divorce, but lectured from the pulpit about her as a fallen woman. I thought of her as Hester Prynne and sometimes as Isolde, her beautiful pale face with the white hair surrounding. I like to think Emily Dickinson could have been writing about her when she wrote, "Title divine — is mine! / The Wife — without the Sign! / Acute Degree — conferred on me — / Empress of Calvary!"

When she wrote about her son's death, she said, "Lips wet with wormwood will not kiss the rood. / I found, instead, a granite bed — / The tomb of solitude." The poem went on to say, "How many mothers to the tomb have fled, / Even as I, alone with Death to brood, / Each finding she was with a multitude."

I read Rupert Brooke and Allan Seeger and Wilfred Owen.

•

In New York, the trees on Riverside Drive were bare in winter. There were bedbugs in the penthouse tenement apartment where Meg and I stayed. When you turned on the light suddenly, you could see them, blackish red and round. Squish and there was a bright perfect red circle on the sheet. You itched for days and days where they bit. Max was on the WPA artist project. He drew line drawings of faces and nudes and was just back from Paris, where he had been discovered by Leo Stein. He told me he had never seen his mother sit down at the table with the family and he would not know her face. He told me he wouldn't marry for love but for the texture of a woman. I waited for him to come over every evening, but when he found I was a virgin, he didn't come over very often.

Meg and I ate croissant and creamed spinach about three times a week at a little restaurant four blocks from Columbia. Every other week we went to Carnegie Hall to see Toscanini. We sat in the gallery and collected beautiful faces. We liked the curves in the lower eyelids of Jewish girls.

Meg introduced me to Yeats. "Nor dread nor hope attend / A dying animal; / A man awaits his end / Dreading and hoping all; / Many times he died, / Many times rose again. / A great man in his pride / Awaiting murderous men / Casts derision upon / Supersession of breath; / He knows death to the bone — / Man has created death."

She introduced me to all her fellow exchange students from England. I went to restaurants with sentimental Hungarians who wept as the singer sang, "Adieu, mein kleiner Garde-Offizier Adieu, Adieu, / Adieu, und vergiss mich nicht und vergiss mich nicht."

Somewhere in the background we knew of Hitler. Jim came down weekends from Princeton. He did not want to go back to England. He was sure war was coming. He would go into deep depressions. He and Meg would stay in her room all Sunday. When he left, she would be depressed too.

•

My sister claimed later that she had asked the question, but I think I had. Of our grandmother. Our grandfather was German. Every few years they would visit Aunt Adele in Fürth. They would bring us Steiff toys, striped tigers and donkeys and, when we were a little older, felt dolls that looked like real children. You could tell they were Steiff by the metal trademark in the ear. "Which side do you hope wins, Granny?" I remember asking. Our grandmother had the saddest smile when she answered. I realized that I had known it was a cruel question even before I asked. That's when I started to hate war. "I'd rather not say," she said. Years later when we told our mother, she wouldn't believe us. "In those days of anti-German feeling to say such a thing to children?" she said. During the war, we were not allowed to play the gramophone record with all the national anthems on it.

I was glad my father had flat feet and also that he couldn't learn to march and was never called up.

On the morning of the False Armistice, the children on the block had a parade. There were five of us, I think. The boys banged on pans for drums. Ethel and I wore our Red Cross nurses' costumes. I thought Red Cross nurses were called that because they were cross like our nurses.

•

They told Margy, "Your mother won a prize in a police raffle." Davy rode his bike home to tell me. Becky said, "Tell them Mom's not home." They waited in front in unmarked cars. None of us spoke about being scared. They'd come for Loretta in the middle of the night and no one to stay with the children. The women in the PTA divided into those who would say "Hello" when I saw them in the neighborhood and those who wouldn't greet me. I went around the block three times before I could make myself go into the low school building with the posters of traffic boys and houses with smoke coming out. Before the meeting, the women were standing around the rostrum. Mrs. Monroe greeted me with her standard smile, Mrs. Finch with a quick noncommittal one. The others pretended not to see me.

The night before the demonstration I told Dave I was scared. He said, "Everyone's scared. It just matters what you *do*."

•

We were lucky, I guess, that we could get away that summer. Leo phoned from New York to say he had rented a house at the Cape, and we piled the kids into the car and drove across the country to join him. We sat in the sand and swam in the ocean and in freshwater pools, and I said to myself, When you remember this summer you will say it was so happy — the dunes, the large house where the grownups would take turns each week with the master bedroom and we teased Ethel because she wouldn't let us change the sheets. And the women took turns getting up with the children in the mornings, and once I was half asleep and was pouring Southern Comfort on the children's pancakes till my nephew said, "Aunt Edith, what are you doing?" And Becky and I lay on the beach and read *Antony and Cleopatra*, and Margy had her first date with a boy and a crush on a very Cape Codish brown-limbed older girl who taught the Red Cross life-saving classes. And Margy was very sullen all summer. And Margy and Becky and I all had our hair cut and looked pretty and conventional, and I looked young. And Becky wouldn't get up in the mornings and stayed in Provincetown till late every night and was very mad at all the boys her age because they were gay. And Dave was mad at Becky because she wouldn't get up in the mornings. And Davy cried very loud and much too long whenever he got hurt, and he scared a little girl by saying there were stingrays in the water, and her mother got mad. And Leo told me children who danced a lot were often schizophrenic, and my children danced a lot. And Rachel stood on the beach and combed Anzy's hair. She was just tall enough to reach it when Anzy was sitting down. And Anzy kept making love to her new husband on the beach, and Jeff was jealous and misbehaved. And Rachel hid under the bed when Leo tried to put drops in her eyes, and when he tried to coax her out and then pull her out, she went further and further under it, and it was low and Leo couldn't reach her.

•

During World War II, all the young mothers took Red Cross classes in first aid. Dorothy and I took turns taking care of each other's babies. When Jaime de Angulo, the anthropologist, cut his wrists, Helen Gibb, who was his sister-in-law and much older than any of us, accompanied him in the ambulance. She told us afterwards that the whole time she kept saying to herself, "I should let him bleed, he's such a bastard, I should let him die, but it's awfully good practice using pressure points."

I sent Meg clothes that my children weren't wearing and a food package and a shirt of Dave's. Although he was heavy then, it was even too big for him and much too long in the arms. Meg told me later that they tried to visualize him from the shirt. They thought he must have arms like a gorilla. She cut it up and made nightgowns for Claire and Judy. Jim was working for the government in food research.

•

Neruda wrote of Stalingrad, "That was the winter / The women held grief / Like hot coals against their breasts," and Hikmet's poems were sneaked out of Turkish prisons. And all the time social hope sustained us, and I must remember to record the vision.

•

Everyone thought Dorothy and I looked alike. Tweedledum and Tweedledee, crazy huge Myrto used to call us at the little Bohemian nightclub she ran. Dorothy wore her hair pulled back and rolled in a bun. She plucked her eyebrows so they went up at an acute and dramatic angle. Dave and Mike were in the merchant marine. Mike loved Hemingway and did not fear death. When he came home from his last trip in the Atlantic theater, he wouldn't talk about it. He couldn't cross streets or go to the barbershop unless Dorothy accompanied him. He wouldn't see us, but once I caught sight of him crossing a street with Dorothy. His hair had turned gray. Four years later he died suddenly. The autopsy showed nothing. Dorothy remarried and I didn't see her for a long time.

•

Because the fog was so thick, the small chartered plane circled London for five hours. When we finally landed, Scotland Yard met us at the airport. They told us the Peace Congress would not be held in Sheffield. They held us incommunicado over night. We sat in a waiting room. They called us up individually. They had a dossier on each of us. It was set on the rostrum separating the person being questioned from the interrogator. I heard the man from Scotland Yard tell Jackie to empty her purse or he would have a matron search her forcibly. I was shaking very badly, and I noticed Holland stayed completely calm. I went to the ladies' room and flushed Meg's address down the toilet. Next day I called Meg from Paris saying I wouldn't be seeing her. I had never been away from my children before, and Rachel was only three, and I had promised Margy I'd be home for her eighth birthday.

The congress was held in Warsaw in a long hall. Every twenty feet there stood a tall statue of a woman with the Picasso peace bird on her wrist. The Korean women spoke to the women on our delegation of their anguish. We promised to take back their stories.

Warsaw was still half rubble. We walked through the rubble of the ghetto and around the immense stone figures on the monument to the ghetto uprising. Bernal, the English physicist, spoke to us, and Joliot-Curie, and I had a chance to talk to Pablo Neruda with the help of a translator, and I told him how the beauty of his poems even survived translation, and he said, yes, he understood they did in English, but they did not come through in every language.

•

There were about three years when I was stuck in the house constantly with a sick child. Davy would get a cold first, then Margy, then the baby, then Becky from taking care of the baby. Each cold would last a week, and then the cycle would begin again. Dave worked on labor defense. Taft-Hartley, McCarran acts. He went to Montana. He went to New York. He went to Arizona. Three weeks a trip. When I met him at the airport, I couldn't find his eyes.

•

When Dave was working nights on the waterfront, Rachel was the only child who was still at home. Sometimes she and I would meet him for midnight lunch. We would drive to the Embarcadero where the entrance to Pier 33 was a plank of light, sit in the parked car and watch the lift-jitneys maneuver inside the gate.

At 12:00 o'clock, we watch the black-jeaned longshoremen saunter out, their steel hooks shining as the street lights hit them. Then we vie to see who will spot him first. He walks out laughing and talking and looking very big and husky, and the men are laughing and talking, and their white caps have smudges of dirt on them, and when Dave sees us he calls "Hello" and smiles, and the men in his gang call "Hello" and greet Rachel, and Dave says goodbye to them, and Hal comes with us and gets in the back seat, and Rachel climbs over to join him, and he puts his arm around her, and she says, "What are you working tonight, Hal, hides?" and he pushes her away and laughs and says, "Hides! I'll give you *hides*, Rachey, I don't smell that bad!" The dusty smell of the docks. The excitement of the wide-awake night when the rest of the town sleeps.

●

Dave and I talked a lot those days about politics and war and what was happening on both sides of the cold war, and we thought about those lines of Brecht that said, "Alas, we / Who wished to lay the foundations of kindness / Could not ourselves be kind," and I grew to hate those lines. And I found myself thinking about Keats' letter to Benjamin Bailey and how he wrote, "I know of nothing but the holiness of the heart's affection . . . ."

●

It wasn't until Judy married Bernal's son and came to America and was about to have her baby in Berkeley that I finally saw Meg again. We sat in Judy and Martin's flat on the south side of the campus, and we kept Judy company as she timed her pains. I left about 5:00, and Meg phoned the next day to say the baby was born at midnight. Martin named her Sophie after Sophia because he had been reading *Tom Jones*.

●

The beginning of the vision: we pledge our lives that Sperry and Bordoise have not laid down their lives in vain. The rainy cemetery and the thousand or so gathered there after the long march up Market Street.

Forty thousand workers marching. No noise except the soft, hushed sound of feet. No police or National Guard in sight. Bare-headed longshoremen dressed in black suits, their hats held behind their backs. At intervals a band plays the Red Funeral March and then is still. My cousin and I stand on the sidelines. She says, "I am going to march." I join her. We hope our fathers are not watching. Last night the newspaper headlines read, "Blood floods the gutters as police and strikers battle on Rincon Hill." Now Nick Bordoise, the cook from Crete, on his way to help in the strikers' kitchen, and Howard Sperry, the longshoreman, lie on these trucks beneath a profusion of flowers.

●

In Galway, the cowherd said, "He just owned the tower and the cottages. My father owned the land across the way. I was born in '39, the year he died." ("Too long a sacrifice / Can make a stone of the heart. / O when may it suffice?") He said, "My father said he was different from the other old men around here. He walked around talking to himself, writing his poems."

Maude Gonne had been angry with him for what she considered his very moderate support of the Easter Rebellion. Years later he proposed to her adopted daughter, Iseult. It was shortly after that he met his wife and began to use her as a medium.

Thoor Ballylee is made of stones from the gorge. The stones are gray, and a greenish-yellow moss creeps up the side visible from the road. Rooks dart in and out of the roof. Meg and I stand on the bank of the stream behind the tower and think of "the cold and rook-delighting heaven."

We come back to the road and ask the cowherd if he will let Dave take a picture of him with the tower as background.

We say goodbye to Meg and watch the train pull out of the little railroad station. I think of a poet's summer place on the Isla Negra, of the collection of mastheads and the wooden breasts of their women and of how ten days after his death the Chilean ruffians destroyed his house and the ornaments of his soul.

IN THE WINGS OF THE JUMP

The jacket had disappeared. I remembered it as brown. I called it my brown tweed jacket, but I could not visualize it. It was gone from my mind's eye as if the idea of the jacket could not exist without the jacket itself. Though I could not picture it, I knew very well what I liked about it. I could recall how it fit tight under my breasts like the cream-colored ribbed silk vest I wore with my riding habit when I was a girl. The vest had yellowed eventually, and the stains had deprived it of all its elegance. When I was still younger, I had a red hunting jacket, a velvet jockey cap, and white duck riding breeches that had to be washed every time I wore them because of the saddle stains and stains down the legs from the horse's sweat, and because of the horse smell as well. I have always liked horse smell, even the smell of manure, the damp hay brine of it, the smell of saddles and bridles with the salty horse saliva on on them, on the different bits — snaffle and curb and the link snaffle used for jumping.

This spring when I took Stephan and Miranda to the horse show at Bercut Field to watch the jumping events, I noticed the style of the riders had changed. They do not stand in the stirrups with their bodies parallel to the horses' backs the way we used to do as soon as we were within the wings of the jump. Once you were in those white-washed wings, you knew the jig was up. Until then you fought the horse, trying to hold him back so he would not approach too fast to gauge his take-off. But when you were in the wings, it was you and the horse together, or rather, it was the horse, and you must do nothing to hinder him. If you were lucky and he was good, there was that wonderful soaring feeling, his muscled withers rising behind you, your distributed weight resting on the outstretched, strong neck. Sometimes right up to the bars, and he'd refuse. Then you knew all you needed to know about incertitude, about accident, about frailty of human plan.

Stephan, sitting on the lowest row of the bleachers and across the aisle from me, was trying to impress a teenage girl. Although I could tell she was not much older than he, she towered over him. I heard the end of a tall tale about rattlesnakes and guns and daring. "Isn't that true, Miranda?" he asked, turning to his sister for confirmation, and Miranda, looking cross and wise with the spurious maturity of the preadolescent, looked down at her raggedy tennis shoes, scuffed them on the tanbark and said, "No."

•

What I have not recorded is that I became absolutely obsessed with the lost jacket. I reviewed every place I had been. I went through every closet in the house, and then I had Dave go through each one again. That only made it worse because the sense of disorder was exacerbated by what seemed to me the disorderliness of the closets: my own closet with the old clothes I do not wear but cannot seem to give away, even the gold Chinese silk hostess pajamas from my college days, and in the hall closet, a down comforter that I have intended to have re-covered for the last seven years, since the feathers began to come out. My sister, Ethel, gave it to me thirty-six years ago when her mother-in-law died. There were two comforters. She had one covered in blue taffeta for herself and one in tan for me. I do not know what happened to hers since she died eleven years ago. I wanted to have mine re-covered in blue taffeta, but I have not been able to find any that can be used for quilting. So it has been lying in the hall closet ever since, beneath Dave's denim, flannel-lined longshore jacket, some place mats I have been meaning to give to Rachel, a torn white wool stole someone left at a party, a black and brown cotton umbrella I bought in the marketplace in Santa Margherita the summer before last.

When I say the jacket became an obsession, I do not use the term lightly. I continued, it is true, to do the housework, see friends, try to read, but always, like a ground base or some prediction of doom, the absence of the jacket throbbed in my head. And with it all, the preoccupation was not made more endurable by the rational knowledge that I had an Irish sweater that was fully as warm or that I could, as I told myself, afford to buy a new one.

Each morning when I woke, I lay in bed and retraced my steps for the days between the time I found it missing and when I had last worn it. This took some figuring, too. It could have been lost for weeks before the Thursday I went to look for it in the closet in my bedroom and found it gone, so I had to establish when I last wore it. By going through each day systematically, I then remembered wearing it to my check-up at Dr. Levin's. I called his office to see if it was in the examining room and called again to see if the nurse had really looked. The second time she replied tartly, "Both the secretary and I think you had it on when you left."

Then one morning about two weeks later, I was lying in bed, half between sleeping and waking and going through what was now my ritual of misery, when suddenly I recalled the Chinese restaurant where we had gone for dinner after seeing *The Great Santini*. I remembered wearing the jacket, because I recollected the feeling of its tweedy stiffness and how uncomfortable that was in the theater and also the particular dust smell of tweed. I dialed the restaurant — I was in a state of great excitement before it opened — and a young woman answered the phone. "Yes," she said, in answer to my question, "we have a jacket. It's been here quite a long time. But it's kind of red with tan and brown below." I thought she meant there were three bands of color — first red, then tan, then brown — but my excitement did not let up. I ran to my car and drove fast through Golden Gate Park. Entering the door through the red and gold tassles and not waiting to come to a halt, I called, "I just phoned you about a jacket." The young Chinese waitress was wiping the salt and pepper shakers. "The one I told you about is hanging on the coat rack inside the kitchen door," she said, indicating the direction with a motion of her head. There it was! A red tweed jacket with tan and brown threads visible within the weave. It was the way I could not remember it, somehow tawdry, with a food spot flattening the rough wool on the left sleeve near the wrist and, inside, a label sewn into the vertical seam saying "100% wool, Made in Italy, Dry Clean Only."

I was, though, tremendously relieved. The world seemed orderly again. But I was also angry with the jacket and dissatisfied, as if a teenage child had run away and you found him and brought him home and you were happy because he was back but you would never quite get over his running away and what that had meant.

•

"He's dead," Ethel said, standing in the sunny garden in Piedmont opposite the graveyard on Moraga Drive, where the family had rented a house in order to spend the summer months away from San Francisco fog. The smell of wisteria seemed to replace the very air itself. The purple blooms leaned luxuriantly out from the vines clinging to the house. The smell is associated in my mind with a peculiar cessation of time I always experience when the weather is hot, as if there were a moratorium on change until the heat is over. Perhaps it is for this reason that the events of the summer stand in particular relief. Uncle Leny had enlisted. Uncle Leny was young and slender and had a thick brown mustache with coarse hairs threading down over his upper lip, and he flirted with me in a way that made me feel grown-up and loved and charming, not just loved the way my parents loved me, but in a special manner that allowed me, while still being a little child, a strange excitement of anticipation. When he went off, my mother said, "Always remember it's the Kaiser. We do not hate the German people."

It was also the summer that my Aunt Gertz died. The way I found out was that all through June and July whenever anyone spoke of my cousins Dick and Roger, who lived in Boston, they mentioned Aunt Madie and not their mother. One day I was playing on the floor, following some numbered dots and watching a figure emerge, when I said to my mother, "How come no one speaks of Auntie Gertz when they talk about Dick and Roger? Is she dead or something?" And I remember glancing up sideways to where my mother sat smocking a dress for my sister. "Yes," she said and turned her head more closely to the gingham yoke on her knee.

Ethel and I were improvising a play. We stood on the lawn just out of reach of the sprinkler. She was the messenger. "He's dead," she said. I was two and a half years younger and a little cowed by her, but not enough to sacrifice a happy ending for our drama. "No," I retorted, "I just got word that the report is mistaken." My sister, unwilling to abandon her ending, with all its tragic glory, became a third messenger who reiterated the dire news. I produced another and she, still another, until defeated and dejected, I broke up the play with my tears.

•

When I was a girl in college, I found a line in Robinson Jeffers I have not been able to locate since. It says, as I remember it, "Good to cry, who can be comforted." Fairly late in life, I came to realize that, in fact, for all that counts there is no comforting. It was about this time that I could no longer cry and I began to wrestle with the concept of death, and my own death became obscured in my mind by fear of the death of those I loved.

For most of my life I have been preoccupied with death. There was a long caesura during the years I was active in the Movement. Whether the let-up resulted from the belief in a socialist future without war where personal mortality became subsumed in superpersonal goals, whether it was an adjunct of the intrinsic optimism of raising young children, an optimism that overrides the dingy idiocy of domestic life, I do not know. But until the time when we experienced the failure of social hope, the fear subsided.

The preoccupation began when I was about ten. That winter we traded houses with Aunt Agnes, who had recently been widowed. We lived on her estate in San Mateo while she took over our house on Clay Street. And with her estate we took over the ménage of cook and gardener. My father had always wanted to live in the country, and this was to be an experiment. It was a bad time, however. My mother was on the edge of a deep depression, and the isolation from city living plunged her into its depth. Although she was far too private to confide in a small daughter, I sensed her unhappiness. In the tree-darkened quiet of the San Mateo nights, I though of her sadness and imagined she was about to die. In my mind, the imminence of her death was associated with her sadness, and I lay awake plotting what I could do to make her happy.

Every weekday, I commuted by train to a girls' school in Palo Alto. Each afternoon, I rushed home from the station, quickly changed from the uniform of middy and skirt, ran up the long driveway to where Maneo, the gardener's son, had his horse tied up against the shed that served as barn. I remember his high Italian coloring against his black hair, how handsome he looked, and the dusty male smell of an eleven-year-old boy. Some days when I arrived, he had the little bay gelding already saddled and bridled. On others, we led him to the fence, exchanged the halter for a bridle, and Maneo held him as I used a slat for stirrup or I held him as Maneo vaulted onto his bare back. Then we took turns cantering him down the long expanse of lawn leading to Aunt Agnes' mansion, where the sour, borrowed cook looked out with disapproval. One day when I had invited Maneo to dinner, she refused to serve him in the dining room, so he and I ate in the kitchen. Soon after, Maneo's father scolded us for tearing up the grass with hoofmarks, and Maneo seemed to lose interest.

After that, I went alone to where the horse stood munching his hay in the small corral, led him to the fence, and tied the halter to the post. I remember how he threw his head sideways against the restraint, how I curried the matted hair his sweat had pasted against the flank, combed the weeds and burrs from the shaggy fetlocks, combed the stiff black mane. I remember the soft muscular feel of his nostrils as I closed them with my left hand and slipped the curb into his mouth, the rough feel and smell of the army saddle blanket, the prickly rope cinch, and how the little horse grunted and expelled air as I thrust my knee against the expanded belly and pulled the cinch tight. Then I was off down the twisty dirt driveway, feeling the motion of horse and the wind pull my long hair till it flew like streamers behind me. And I plotted how I could get my mother to take up horseback riding.

•

"The body (*soma*) is the tomb (*sema*) of the soul." An apothegm opened every lesson. Mr. Allen explained the play on words. He had written the text himself. The second lesson began with "A sound mind is heaven's greatest gift."

It was known that Mr. Allen's own son was severely retard-ed. A large adolescent, he wandered about the Berkeley neighborhood surrounding his home. Mr. Allen's expres-sion was very sorrowful and portentous when he had us translate the saying. Three days a week I rushed down the Rose Street steps to my eight o'clock Greek class. The fol-lowing year we studied Homer: "Sing, Goddess, the wrath of Achilles, Peleus' son, that brought to the Achaeans woes innumerable." When we read *The Apology*, Mr. Linforth in-sisted on a literal translation: "The fear of death, O gentle-men, nothing is but to pretend to know that which we do not know . . . I know that I do not know."

•

It must have fallen out of a book I pulled from the shelf last week, a dingy piece of paper bearing material evidence to what I had long domesticated into my private mytho-logy. It is the kind of receipt you can still buy in any five-and-dime. It reads: Date — June 25, 1934   Donor — Anonymous   Amount — $25.00, and it is signed MWIU.

Summer 1934: the San Francisco waterfront is closed down. A long and bloody strike has divided the city. In middle-class homes the family is sharply divided, so that dinner tables are barricades — mothers and children on the side of the strikers, businessmen fathers on the side of the employers. Greta and I, with money borrowed from my mother, have taken the cable car to the foot of California Street to the headquarters of the Marine Workers' Industri-al Union.

Summer 1932: Greta, my mother, and I are at Lake Ta-hoe. Greta has worked for the family for eight years, since she was nineteen and I was eleven. She had grown up in Germany during World War I, and she inherited from her childhood thin rickety legs, a consuming hatred of war and a passion for social justice, a passionate dedication to learning.

She had never had a real childhood. When she first came to work for us, she liked to play catch with me in our back yard at Clay Street, where when I was younger I had rubbed myself with the gray gravel that covered the path and said, "Look, Aunt Madie, I am an elephant." Later, she worked out a schedule with my mother that permitted her to go to school three days a week.

I am an indifferent student. I feel guilty because she has to struggle very hard for something I seem to throw away. The winter before we go to Lake Tahoe, Greta has fallen in love with Heinrich, a communist she has met in the German hiking club on Mount Tamalpais. At a rented summer house at Lake Tahoe, Greta is telling my mother and me that you cannot abolish war without abolishing capitalism. My mother and I know nothing about politics or political theory. We argue evolution. Greta argues revolution. At the end of the discussion, we come to a united front. We are all against war. The measure of sincerity is action.

Fall 1932: I return to college and join the antiwar movement. It is a bright September day on the campus of the University of California in Berkeley. Lou Goldblatt is debating Oleta O'Connor. She says the League for Industrial Democracy will not form a united front with the National Student League against War and Fascism unless the organization renounces class war as well as imperialist war. Lou says being against class war is like being against death: it will still exist. I join the National Student League.

•

"April is the cruellest month, breeding / Lilacs out of
the dead land . . . " I read *The Waste Land* as an antiwar
poem. My new Marxist friends say the only criterion for
judging a work of art is whether it advances the interests of
the proletariat. It is in the interest of the working class to
have peace. Eliot lectures at the University of Virginia. He
says, " . . . reasons of race and religion combine to make
any large number of free-thinking Jews undesirable." My
new friends say there is no disjunction between the writer's
life and his work. "Webster was much possessed by death /
And saw the skull beneath the skin; / And breastless crea-
tures underground / Leaned backward with a lipless grin /
. . . Grishkin is nice; her Russian eye / Is underlined for emphasis; / Uncorseted, her friendly bust / Gives promise of
pneumatic bliss / . . . And even the abstract entities / Cir-
cumambulate her charm;/ But our lot crawls between dry
ribs / To keep our metaphysics warm." The movement was
Eros. Eliot was Thanatos.

•

Becky joins a delegation of white and black students
who request the principal to schedule an observance of
Negro History week. Mr. Hunter is adamant. "If you bring
attention to these things," he says, "you just make them
worse. Take the position of the Jews in World War II. I
heard so much about their suffering, and it just made me
mad at them."

When Paul Robeson comes to town, he will no longer
stay in a downtown hotel. He reserves a room at the Booker

T. Washington in the Fillmore. He meets with the black
trade unionists from the longshoremen's union and sup-
ports their plan for a black labor caucus. When he comes to
visit us, there is the old warmth, but there is a new tension.
Davy sings a song he has learned in Boys' Chorus and is
very happy about Paul's approval.

Rosalee McGee tours the country on behalf of her husband, who is under sentence of death because a white
woman, enraged at his rejection of her sexual advances,
has accused him of rape.

•

Rachel is eight the summer we join Dave in Stockton,
where he is working on the waterfront in order to get his
membership book in the longshore union. Becky and
Margy are studying dance in Utah. Davy is in music camp.
Dave is taking a break from the labor defense work that has
kept him on the road six months of the year during the Mc-
Carthy attacks.

The previous winter, the children and I stayed in San
Francisco. Dave usually came home Fridays, arriving just as
the children were leaving for school. At first we felt glad to
see each other, but inevitably during the weekend we began to quarrel. Dave scolded the children for not helping
enough with the housework, and I would grow angry at his
takeover when I had the responsibility all week.

Some weekends I met him in Stockton, where he
boarded in Hotel Milner on the skid row. We walked
through the peering glances of the old men in the dingy
lobby that smelled of fumigation like rundown movie
houses, and we tried to make love in a single bed with

saggy springs. Or we treated ourselves to dinner and two martinis at a shiny restaurant with an old bar and dark woodwork and a tough and friendly waitress. Then, feeling good and oblivious to the prospect of the tawdry room, we looked forward to going to bed. But sometimes before I was undressed, Dave had fallen into a deep sleep. Next morning he would be abashed and apologize as he put me on the Greyhound for San Francisco.

In June we rent our house in San Francisco to some skaters from the Ice Follies, and Rachel and I join Dave in a bungalow he has sublet. It is the summer after Khrushchev's report to the Twentieth World Congress, and we are in a mood of shock and bewilderment at the revelations of Stalin's crimes.

In the hot Stockton nights when I talk my way past the guards on the army docks to bring Dave his midnight lunch which he has forgotten, in the sweltering afternoons beside the public pool, I brood about our lives and how we had failed to see what was happening in the USSR, and I brood about the slavishness of our own Movement.

•

Dave had become acquainted with the Stockton library in the winter he spent alone, and now he brings us records from their collection. The three of us listen to them together in the daytime, and Rachel and I listen to them in the humid nights when he is working. He introduces us to Edith Sitwell's *Facade* with music by Sir William Walton and to the songs of John Dowland and Purcell. Rachel likes to go to sleep with the phonograph playing "Music for a while." I sit in the hot living room with the door open to the front yard and the door open to Rachel's room and the tenor's voice singing, "Music fo-o-or a-a while / Will all your cares beguile / Will all, will all, will all, will all your cares beguile." I think in some way it was the listening to those records over the political counterpoint in my mind that determined me to return to college and the studies I had left behind in order to embark upon an activist life.

•

In the late afternoon, Rachel and I accompany Dave to the wooden hiring hall beside the railroad track. Rachel goes in with him to see whether he will be dispatched. Dave likes to work in a gang with Whitey Rhodes and Biggie, the tall old lumberstiff, and Blackie. On a work night as they emerge from the hall, I hear Rachel ask Biggie what cargo they will be handling. She knows that barley fibers get all over your clothes and dust gets in your nose. She knows the difference between bulk and containerized cargo. The men are amused by the little girl who is so expert about the industry, and they are very tender with her.

On a night where there is no work, Biggie invites us to a barbecue. We enter through the house where he and Aggie are preparing a potato salad and walk out to the patio Biggie has laid. The fire is already smouldering in the open grate. I sit and talk with Ida, who is a beautician. She complains about her husband, Blackie, the handsome, swashbuckling half Cherokee. Rachel thinks he looks like Clark Gable and loves him with all her little girl passion until one night he rants against "niggers." "Daddy," she whispers loudly into Dave's ear, "is he on our side?" Biggie is still in the house cooking, I hear him yell at Aggie to get out of his way. "Nobody tells me to get out of the way in my own kitchen," she says. That evening she sits and chats with the other wives in the patio. Biggie prepares dinner.

•

The next winter I went back to college. Rachel resented my not being home school afternoons even though she had activities every day but Wednesday. "I don't care," she said, in answer to my remonstrance, "I like the idea of your being there whether I am or not." But I could not concentrate in my own house although there was no one around in the daytime, for the house, itself, scolded and derided if any work was undone. So I would go across town to my sister's and hole up in a bedroom that had belonged to my nephew before he left for university. It was there that I studied Milton again after so many years in which I had repudiated all such reading, and I mused, in my retreat, on his injunction against "a fugitive and cloistered virtue." It was there that I wrestled with Hart Crane and his metaphysics of meaninglessness. It was there that I began to evaluate Marxist aesthetics and to try the rarefied air of the New Critics. In resuming a life I had turned my back upon twenty years before, I found excitement and nourishment. Yet there was no way I could cease to grieve for the system of belief I had lost, nor would I in any manner abjure the social goals that had led me into the Movement.

Dave had his book in the union now and worked nights out of the San Francisco longshore local. Weekdays our schedule meshed well. Weekends, however, the noise of children playing in front of the house woke him. He would get out of bed, huge and furious, charge down the stairs with only an undershirt on and the evening paper held in front of his genitals and stand on the front porch shouting in indignation.

•

The year I was hired to teach at the trade campus of the community college in Oakland was the same year that the House Committee on Un-American Activities sent an advance team to investigate teachers in California. The investigators completed their work in the spring. I did not sign a contract till midsummer. Consequently, when the subpoenas were served in the fall, I was not among those called.

Hearings were held in the San Francisco City Hall. For the first time in all the McCarthy years, they did not proceed unopposed. Hundreds of students crowded the corridors demanding entrance to the chambers. When ordered to leave, they refused. The police attacked with fire hoses and washed them down the steep marble stairs. On my return home from school, I found Becky was in jail and Margy was nursing a sprained ankle.

•

When you have been a housewife for seventeen years and you go to a job, it is a bit like going to a masquerade except that the mask also faces inward. Who am I before this class? I wonder daily. Where is that other self, attentive to the least demand? (Button to be sewn on, work clothes to be ready, school lunch to be made. "No, Mother, nobody carries a lunch bag like that to school." I have run out of brown bags and put the sandwich and fruit and cookies in a bread wrapper. "Mother, I have to have a Halloween costume, and if it is like anyone else's, it'll be awful.") Where is that other self, geared always for emergencies? In the middle of the night, Dave is home early from his shift, his face bloodied, his nose swollen, two teeth knocked out from where a 700-pound cotton bale has fallen from the top of the wagon he was loading in the hold of the ship.

During this period, the trade campus is being converted into a comprehensive college. I am one of the first academics to be hired. Amid the suspicion and mistrust of the trade faculty, my way is made easier because it is known on the grapevine that my husband is a longshoreman. When I am called in by the dean and the president to answer charges concerning Dave's alleged subversive activities, they are embarrassed and ill at ease. They assure me of their liberalism. I assure them that the charges are without doubt accurate. They tell me my tenure will not be affected. When I think about it later, I realize that they were attempting to warn me of forces over which they ultimately had no control.

The sheet metal workshop is across from my classroom. We are reading Yeats' prayer for his daughter: "My mind, because the minds that I have loved, / The sort of beauty that I have approved / Prosper but little, has dried up of late . . . " There is a thundering noise as if a huge building has toppled in an earthquake. I start. The students laugh and explain that the semester's supply of sheet metal has been delivered.

The plumbing instructor flunks all black students until the president demands to see the examination papers. The carpentry instructor, an old Marxist and a philosopher, tells his students, "Study the humanities. A man or woman must never be a mule."

A

Several of the works read this semester
define the meaning or value of life at the
moment in which existence, itself, is
threatened and at which death is confronted. Compare and contrast the attitudes of
the protagonists towards the fact and
meaning of death and life at the moment of
confrontation. Support your arguments by
evincing close knowledge of the works
considered.

B

Discuss the following statement: A central
problem in *Hamlet* and in *No Place to Be
Somebody* is whether one has to become
that which one hates in order to defeat that
which one hates. Compare and contrast
the position of Hamlet, the humanist
scholar in the court of Claudius, with that
of Gabe, the black intellectual in the East
Village bar in the Sixties.

C

In the process of achieving a sense of iden-
tity and reaching one's goals, each person
goes through a period in which the self is
made a stranger or is perceived a stranger
from a former context — an environment,
a past, a family, a former self. The process
may be initiated by external events, but
when it is recorded in literature

the interest lies in the consciousness and the course of the person undergoing the alienation . . . how the protagonist separates herself or himself, gradually or suddenly, from what has gone before, what unrest or anguish is suffered during the period of withdrawal, and eventually, the resolution of the spiritual journey. Discuss Meursault in *The Stranger* and Edna in *The Awakening* in relation to the above concept.

•

"We will grind the wheels of this institution to a halt," the students said, using the threat made famous by Mario Savio in the free speech fight at the University of California a few years earlier. The convocation was called for noon in the auditorium of the Grove Street campus. All classes were canceled. The shabby halls were empty. From the rostrum, speaker after speaker spoke eloquently, demanding courses in black studies, demanding meal tickets, book loans, an increase in black and Third World faculty. Speaker after speaker shouted grievances against the racist society that conducted a white college in the midst of the Oakland ghetto. "If you whites are sleeping nights," a student shouted over the loudspeaker, "we blacks are not doing our job." I was glad, I told myself for the militancy and the proud consciousness, though when I recounted the speech to Rachel, the only child still at home, she said wryly, "By you, Mom, they are doing their job" but I was not glad to be hated for my white skin nor to be excluded from

74

a cause I had long espoused. A black colleague passed me in the hall daily without a nod of recognition.

The classrooms were now charged with energy. Students tried on concepts like badly needed clothing. Words were no longer mere print on a white page but vibrant challenges, calls to action, means of leverage. I thought about the poets I had loved in my youth, the voices of the Negro Renaissance. I remembered the lyrical resigned voice of Countee Cullen: "We shall not always sow while others reap / The golden increment of fallen fruit . . ." I brought to class Claude McKay's fiery sonnet: "If we must die, let it not be like dogs . . ." I had the school library purchase the Paul Robeson recording of *Othello*. The history classes were alive with the discovery of the works of W. E. B. DuBois.

•

For some years before my sabbatical I had been teaching *The Stranger*. Each semester I planned not to. Each semester the book appeared on the assignment sheet with an inevitability that bewildered me. It is a book I really dislike. Starting with Meursault's cold detachment from his mother, continuing through the brutal collaboration with the pimp, Sintés, and culminating in the senseless murder of the Arab, I resent the stance of the author, and resent the eyestrain, so to speak, of seeing through his glasses. Hence it always takes me by surprise when I become aware of my absorption with the second half of the book and note that I spend a good three weeks of class time discussing it. We explore the spatial limits of the cell and the temporal limits imposed by the sentence of death. We watch Meursault ponder every possible avenue of escape, wondering whether the "inevitable admits a loophole," finally knowing there is none but "unable to stomach this brutal certitude." We consider how, at the very last, he remembers for the first time, "with death so near, [how] Mother must have felt like someone on the brink of freedom, ready to start life all over again."

On the airplane to Heathrow, I push the button that allows the seat to recline. I order a drink. It is dark except for the lights marking the exits, the restrooms, and the quarters where the stewardesses rest. I peer out at the black, indistinguishable sky through which we travel. Dave is sitting across the aisle sleeping. He has been to London before and is eager to show me around. I am wide awake, excited about the six-month holiday ahead. Beyond the halfway mark by far of my own life, I muse, "O lente, lente currite, noctis equi!" Suddenly, I am thinking of Meursault's mother and then of Meursault, as if for the first time understanding not with my mind alone how he accepts the limits of the sentence and the cell, lays his "heart open to the benign indifference of the universe." And with a rush of joy, I know, although the time is short, "the interim is mine."

•

Ruth introduces me to the novel *Things Fall Apart* by the Nigerian writer Chinua Achebe. I introduce her to Kate Chopin's *The Awakening*. Though we have very little time together at work, the sharing of the same office allows us quick, welcome exchanges between classes or at the end of conferences with students. Ruth, like me, had come back to her education after raising a family. She had left Vienna in flight from Hitler when she was fifteen, married, had three sons, and enrolled in the community college where she now teaches when her youngest child entered school. We seem to share as well a kind of fallout from our roles of mother and grandmother even as we introduce students to new academic rigors. But in spite of, or perhaps because of, our immediate histories from which we are in part attempting to escape, we rarely form close personal friendships with students.

Ruth rushes into our large disorderly office. It is crowded with six faculty desks, three bookcases, stacks of dittoed hand-out sheets on the shelf that describes the length of the room. She greets me with her wide, curly smile and sometimes a quick hug. She wears what I call her Garbo trench coat, her narrow waist cinched in above the hips that so annoy her. She is going to be late to class. She riffles hurriedly through the large poetry file we have collected in the school-issue metal cabinet.

Some days when I have to stay over for a special evening class, I drive to the house in Oakland hills she and Gil had designed when the boys were young. Ruth has left a key for me behind the PG&E box. I pass the brilliant red maple by the front door. The little dog, Dina, she acquired after Gil's death greets me with a bark and a wagging of the tail so vigorous that it depresses her haunches. I let myself in and fall asleep on the living room couch. The sun beats through the dark blinds that are supposed to moderate its glare.

When Ruth comes in, she pours a Scotch and soda for herself and a vodka for me. She talks about a new course she is teaching in women's studies and an edition of *King*

Lear with a modern English counterface. She speaks of her new friend Bill, who is writing a book on Irish socialism, and her grandson Jeffrey and the new baby Stefanie. I speak of Dave, and Stephan and Miranda, and of Soyinka's version of *The Bacchae*, which I am now teaching. And we talk of the delight in our grandchildren and our guilt that we will not serve as sitters.

On a Saturday, we meet in Dolores Park to protest U.S. intervention in El Salvador. She and Bill have marched up Market Street to the rally. Bill is exhilarated and is shouting slogans. Because Dave's leg is bad, we have driven to the meeting place. When the speeches and collection are finished, we walk over the grassy hill, greet old friends, pass mothers with new babies, young fathers with children on their shoulders. We drive in our car to Lucca's where we buy gnocchi and pesto and tomatoes, a loaf of French bread and a bottle of Pinot Noir. Over dinner at our house, we reminisce about the little remodeled farmhouse at Santa Margherita we had rented for consecutive summers — the drenched blue Tyrrhenian in constant view, our friend Martha and the strange, enormous Gloria Pardini with her marble-floored villa, her long-time lover, whom she called *the little one*, her pet tortoise and his fight with the tortoise belonging to her neighbor, the crown prince. And inevitably we talk about the progress of Ruth's work on the women of the Irish rebellion.

•

When Ruth was in the hospital, I brought some poppies, a meager plant with striped red and yellow petals. Dave had shopped for it that morning. There was not much choice because it was Valentine's Day and the florists were almost sold out. The oxygen tubes were in her nostrils, and her fine Semitic forms seemed accentuated by her loss of weight — the curved delicate nose, the curving lower lids of her eyes, her wide, curly mouth. Her brownish auburn hair against the pillows set off the pale fineness of her skin. I admired a flower arrangement, an impressionist still life of tulips and white roses. Ruth said there was a story behind it. A few months back, needing some stimulation outside the classroom, she had enrolled in an evening course in San Francisco. An old man whom she had met there had taken a fancy to her. When he called her home and Bill picked up the phone, however, he declined to leave his name. She laughed tenderly as she reported telling him it was all right to speak to Bill. After he heard she was in the hospital, he wanted to come to see her, but she was not feeling well enough for a visit; so he had sent the flowers.

Bill had suggested I bring some poetry, as he said Ruth found talking difficult, but I could find none I wanted to read. When I told her, she said, yes, she had tried to find some Emily Dickinson for her mother when she was dying, but her mother had not wanted to listen. I told her the only line I could think to bring her was: "To cease upon the midnight with no pain." "Wouldn't that be wonderful!" she said.

•

From Ruth's journal:
How I wish they would shut off. The obscene 8 million dollars inauguration of

Reagan, the disgustingly archaic military
struttings called "parades" . . . Nuclear
weaponry escalates on both sides of East-
West . . . Somehow knowing of my own im-
minent death does not mitigate the *anger*
and sorrow . . . I do care! And the idiocy of
the avoidable catastrophe infuriates me.

•

Ruth and I discussed death one of the good afternoons
we had together before she put herself in the hospital. She
said she was not afraid of death, since she did not believe
in an afterlife. I did not know, nor did I ask her, why she
did not fear the cessation of breath, the cessation of sen-
tience as I do. We talked about Camus and Sartre, and she
explained the message of "The Wall," which I had always
missed, thinking it lay in the ending. "No," she said, "the
ending is only a trick. The message lies in the acceptance
of death and how the condemned face it the night before
their expected execution." That part, she mused, she
agreed with, but not with the detachment from the living
the story seems to advocate. She said she in no way wanted
to separate herself from those she loved in the face of
death. She spoke of her children and Bill and the grandchildren. Earlier that day she told me she had always been
a great journal keeper, and since she had first received
what she called "the verdict," she had recorded all her experiences of confronting cancer and death. She was glad,
she said, that she had never postponed what she wanted to
do, and although she would have liked to have another ten

years — and then in deference to the fact that I was precisely ten years older than she — or a few more, she was not
afraid of death. I suggested she write her own views on dying, how perhaps a woman facing death is not, like Sartre's
protagonist, willing to forego caring. As it turned out, however, she did not have time.

THE INELUCTABLE SILENCE
OF THE LAKE

I have only the bare bones of the story, picked clean by
time. I cannot summon her physical presence before the
television screen of the mind, but simply, to work the anal-
ogy, can summon up such a description as one might read
of a person missing: Alison Clay. No photograph available.
Approximate height, 5'2". Weight, 102. Age 25. Hair, light
brown. Complexion, fair to olive. Eyes, gray. Customary
manner of dress, tidy, inconspicuous.

I say the story is picked clean by time, but I wonder if
that is true. I have never been able to record in memory
that which I do not understand, and I have never understood Alison or her story. Perhaps I know as much about it
now as I did then. Perhaps my failure to recall her physical
likeness stems from the fact that her appearance gave no
clue to the short trajectory that was to be her life. Not that
she seemed secretive. If she did not use me as a confidante,
well I was what at that time seemed much younger. I was, I
suppose, sixteen when first we met; she, twenty-two or
twenty-three. She must have been at the most twenty-five

when Mr. Carson and I sat in the Little Chapel of the Flowers in Berkeley, I sobbing until my nose and eyes were swollen shut; he, stoic but bereft, clutching my hand in his; before us, the flower-draped coffins.

What are those bare bones, then? And what impels me now, myself close to the dark that she embraced so young, to track her on the sudden trip from Munich to the steep, fatal shores of the Nevada lake?

When I first met Alison she had just returned from a year in Germany, where she had been working on her dissertation. A distinguished student of linguistics, she was something of a protegée of Mr. Carson's, and since I was boarding at his house, I had occasion to see her on her frequent visits, both professional and social. At Mr. Carson's suggestion she had taken under her wing the excited teenager to whom college seemed a borderless world of knowledge and wonder. I think she enjoyed my enthusiasm, for she initiated a series of evening walks. It must have been during the first of these that she encouraged me to register in beginning Greek. "It will be only one year, and you will be starting to read Homer," she said, "and there is nothing to compare with reading the *Iliad* in the original. Keats to the contrary notwithstanding," she added. "Try to get into Rolph Jepson's class," she urged. "He's excellent."

I had hoped that in reconstructing the walks I would trigger some heretofore inaccessible memory and be able to bring to my mind's eye a more corporeal Alison than I was able to conjure above. But all I can see is a small woman with dun-colored hair and skin, a tidy slender body devoid of curves. I remember her quick humor and the gay exchange of glance between her and Mr. Carson as they joked about some academic foolishness or a pretentious colleague — for Alison was at this time a teaching assistant in the German Department.

There had been rumors about Alison and Rolph Jepson before she left for Europe the second time and, ostensibly, for good. I had seen them frequently together on the campus, Rolph tall and gauche, always with a squashed, gray pork-pie hat above his stringy hair, walking with his lurching stride, engrossed in conversation but looking ahead, to one side and then the other and only as if by chance at Alison as she addressed him. I guess I speculated about their relationship, but Alison did not talk to me about her personal life, and I enjoyed our discourse in the realms of knowledge and philosophy, a discourse so different from that of the moody self-absorbed discussions I engaged in with my peers.

It was on one of our walks towards the end of my freshman year, however, that Alison did confide in me, though whether the announcement of plans that were soon to be public constituted a confidence I am not sure. At any rate she announced that she was leaving at the end of the spring semester for Germany, where she would marry Helmuth, an engineer she had met in Berlin during her sojourn at the university the previous year. If she described her fiance, I have no recollection of the description. I do recall a feeling of her certainty about what she was doing and that she regarded the move to Germany as a permanent one. My assumption was that she was in love with Helmuth and considered him as well a congenial partner with whom she anticipated spending her life. I was sad about her leaving. We had formed a very warm friendship, and I regarded her as a kind of link between myself and the awe-inspiring presence of the university. I recall as well that Mr. Carson seemed personally stricken about her departure and that his crepe-soled, shuffling walk became even more shuffling, and his life, always so separate from that of Mrs. Carson, appeared for some days or weeks even more separate, and that he seemed to turn to me for companionship. I do not remember the day she left or how or where we said goodbye.

The semester after Alison departed, I passed Rolph Jepson several times on the walk between Wheeler Hall and Sather Gate. Homer was not being offered that year, so I would have to wait until my junior year for his class, I thought. He would lift his hat to me in his courteous, abstracted way, and I could read nothing in his pale, scholarly face to indicate whether he was suffering. I think I believed him impervious to involvements of the flesh or even, for that matter, of the soul. "I saw that poor chap Rolph today," Mr. Carson remarked, however, one evening over supper, "alone again, always alone."

And that was all. Meanwhile the papers were full of the rise of a little paper-hanger from Munich, his harangues, his appeal to the wounded pride of the German people, his attribution of all evils to the Jews, the communists, the social democrats. And no one heard from Alison.

From the shore of Pyramid lake in the Sierra, one cannot see how swiftly and precipitously the ground recedes, so that waders, surprised, may easily lose their footing. The obituary in the *Berkeley Gazette* afforded no information save the fact of the drownings. Mr. Carson said that he knew Alison could swim, but he was very dubious about Rolph, city-bred and bookish from youth. Perhaps Rolph stepped suddenly over a ledge into the deep waters, and Alison, attempting to rescue him, pulled down by his flailing weight, unwilling to let him go, sank into the frigid mountain lake. Or perhaps, hand in hand and resolute in shared despair, they walked together to where the ground fell suddenly away.

Only the bare bones of the story. If I had hoped retracing it would elicit answers I could not hear or did not dare to hear before, I was wrong. Only the facts remain: the stark Hitler years she would not see and the double drowning. Only the facts and unanswered questions: a new love lost, an older love regained, an accident? or all, all lost and then the voluntary waters?

DISTANCES

This story has been a long time in the making. For many years I could see it only in terms of distances. First there was that subtle distance that had existed between us, all during those close years of our friendship. Then there was the gradual distancing that began in our last years of college. And there was that further distance when she married and became a mother while I lived in a redwood flat on Tamalpais Road, absorbed in my discovery of the politics of the thirties, their visions and injunctions, their scorn of the uncommitted life.

Perhaps this last consideration explains in part the special quality of the distance that lay between us on our last visit. Perhaps it explains in part my failure to perceive the shadow of a headstone, to foresee the unalterable distance into which she was ushered by those strange, funereal parents, who had nurtured and impounded her from birth.

For about two or three times a year after her death and over a period of twenty-five years, I made my obeisance in a recurring dream. It varied but varied only as a story does in the recounting. The essential events remained the same.

The dream: We would meet somewhere, or I would be brought to where she was. She had been dead, she acknowledged, and she was back. But the distance of her death would stand ever between her and the living. And in that dream, the distance was in an indefinable way our loss, not hers.

It was in the year of 1937. Newspapers still carried three-inch headlines, and newsboys hawked extras in the streets. But I cannot remember where I first saw the headlines or how I first knew who the unidentified girl lying in the hospital bed was. The picture showed her with her head swathed in bandages, her mouth slightly open, her gaze that of one in the doorway between consciousness and death. The story said she had climbed to the top of the highest building in San Francisco, made an excuse to the custodian to be admitted to the roof, and jumped the thirty stories that landed her alive but mortally wounded on the pavement below. All identification had been torn from her body in some last agony of self-annihilation, so that neither her coat nor her dress bore the name of the place of purchase. She lived a few hours. She would not or could not reveal her name. But she was heard to murmur a single word that sounded like "baby." I knew better.

To that long and early and long-forbidden relationship that combined in an obscure way all she was, all she could have been, Maxine had brought as well part of what she could not renounce. So that her husband and the father of her child was given the name of *Badey*.

Our last visit had been about three months earlier. It was an autumn afternoon, and she had secured time off from the routine of house and baby. She was living in the city, and I, through a strange ricocheting of circumstance, in a studio apartment in the Berkeley hills across the road and three houses down from the rooms we had occupied as freshmen seven years before. I sat on a couch with my back to the window; she, in a chair where she could look past me to the road where we had walked so many times together and separately to and from classes — rushing for the Euclid Avenue bus in the mornings, strolling back in the quiet green of the late afternoons. She appeared formal now, dressed in her city clothes. I remember that she took off a black pump and massaged her toes, stopping abruptly in the accounting she was giving me of her present life. And I remember the simultaneous feeling of closeness and separation of our lives when she turned toward me suddenly and asked, "Are you happy, now?"

Both of us, we recalled, had felt that freshman year like Keats first looking into Chapman's *Homer.* We boarded in the house of an old professor, who, in the loneliness of a sad marriage, opened up to the two escapees from the last of the all-girls public schools what seemed like endless vistas of learning — music, literature, art, philosophy. These vistas, merging behind our eyes with the verdure of the winding, hilly roads and their warm, human dwellings, were in sharp contrast to the San Francisco we had known. The city at that time had no trees in residential districts, and the gray of pavement and asphalt seemed to form a continuum with the drab high school and the almost total lack of cultural nutriment for two hungry, speculative girls, who sought it out greedily from each other, from a few teachers, from one or two older friends. So that a world centered around learning, a town whose very greenness seemed to symbolize our own spring, was a wondrous thing. There would be evenings when the professor would introduce us to a new symphony on his fine phonograph in the large, audacious living room. Or what seemed the privileged invitation through him to the home of a distinguished colleague. Or a small group gathered to read their poetry at the home of an English instructor.

As I write this, however, I become aware of the distortion of time and the word. Because Maxine and I remembered that we were often depressed. Perhaps that is too strong a description. Perhaps we were just blue. But in the light of ensuing events, our moods and what they signified invite some probing. We were blue because we did not feel adequate. We were blue because we could not ascribe meaning or purpose to life. We were blue because we were mortal. We were often blue and we didn't know why. Mostly we were blue about men — Maxine about Irwin, and I about a shy and unspoken love for a young man who sat behind me in Greek 1A, Monday, Wednesday, and Friday at 8:00 a.m.

Of those distances. Even in high school. Maxine and I discovered each other, but the discovery did not come quickly. In the stultifying halls, in the dank gray of the girls' locker rooms, Maxine's conversation consisted of starts and stops, of trivial, self-interrupting venturings, of adolescent gossip about boys and dances, of halts and self-demeanings. Then suddenly there was that searching, literate paper on *Point Counterpoint,* and the secret was out. The secret and with it the mystery. And her secret became the basis of our friendship. We read poetry, we read novels, we tried to read *Decline of the West.* And we discovered literary criticism and cultivated it with possessive excitement. In the pages of *The Bookman,* we threw ourselves into the controversy between the Naturalists and the Humanists, and under the tutelage of Rebecca West we hailed D. H. Lawrence and scorned Paul Elmer More. And all the while, in the world of schoolmates and social life and family, Maxine played the addlepate.

It is only fair to say that the above description leaves out the incongruities in the development of the observer as well. I hated high school with a determined, unforgiving melancholy that precluded success, and I held on to my hatred with a passion diverted from some other areas. Such as that I was a wallflower. Pretty in a serious way that adults assured me would appeal to older men, I was anathema to the boys at the dances that came around ineluctably every two weeks. And I countered their disregard with a shielding and repelling wit and a refusal to play the game. I know now that the refusal was composed, if unequally, of two elements — a genuine distaste for the boys themselves as well as a rather tardy sexual awakening. As inevitably as the onset of puberty itself, however, all the young of the German-Jewish community were gathered into an orchestrated social life and one for which I was ill-prepared. Ill-prepared by a family who had themselves turned their backs on the arid, prescribed, arrived life of that community. And Maxine had been gathered as unknowingly into the folds of the Polish-Jewish group. I say "unknowingly" because there was no vocal acknowledgement of the affinities or the exclusions before the sudden invitations to the regular dances.

Maxine was very popular at these dances. I don't think she went through the conscious discomfort of concealing her rather extraordinary intelligence. By some quirk in her person, she had the natural ability to mask it and to fill the requisite demands. She could act at once cute and dumb.

She was very pretty as well. A short upper lip with just the faintest shadow of hair emphasized the mobility of her mouth. Her nose avoided the retroussé by virtue of a slight Semitic curve. Her eyes were dark brown, and I remember for some reason that although her lashes were long, they were not curved. Sometimes when she was acting dumb, she would narrow her eyes and open her lips slightly as if she were trying to understand something beyond her depth. But sometimes she would narrow them in a manner of hard appraisal uncomfortably reminiscent of her father's. She was of medium height, slender enough to conform to the fashion of boyish figures. Yet she had high, rounded breasts, of which she had what seemed — to my Puritan and unawakened consciousness — the temerity to be proud.

Maxine, too, hated high school, but she was sustained through that period by her academic success and her acuity at the biweekly dances. And if the front of girlish silliness made her unthreatening to the tentative masculinity of the boys at the dances, it did not conceal from one of those boys her other qualities. Engaged at first by her looks and her vivacity, Irwin, some three years older than she, soon found in her an intelligence and seriousness matching his own. And they fell in love with surprise and wonder and tenderness.

When it came to the attention of her parents that Maxine was involved with Irwin, they were at first concerned, then disapproving. She was the only child of a couple too old and too old-world for their roles. Her father was a first generation American, a doctor. He had achieved considerable fame for his work in cardiology, and he had come up through poverty by dint of single-mindedness. With something of the appearance of a Jewish scarecrow — moustache, hair awry, always in an ill-fitting suit with dandruff sprinkled on collar and shoulder — he moved through life intent on money, professional esteem, on the one hand, and dependent, on the other, on the control and adoration of his daughter, and the back-up of his anonymous, dowdy, slow-talking wife. It seems not without contradiction that the doctor and his wife would expect their daughter not only to go to college but also to live away from home. What their expectations were for her as a result of her education are no more obscure, however, than those of other middle-class parents of college girls of that era. Possibly a career. Probably an appropriate marriage. And Irwin did not seem an appropriate mate.

He was not suitable because his father was a tailor. The doctor was on the next rung up on the American immigrant ladder. Too close still to the world of sweatshop and ghetto. To the nagging of poverty. To the ostracism of accent. Maxine must have known these reasons and must have at some point revealed them to me by indirection. But for the most part they remained quarried in part of her mind, unspoken and unnamed, so that the content of her father's disapproval moved into that realm of distances between us.

The doctor forbade Maxine to see Irwin, and her last year of high school was dominated by the commanded separation and the tortured, infrequent secretive meetings on Irwin's weekend returns from college. As Maxine's friend, I was privy to her pain and perplexity. And I became aware as well of a different element in the prohibition, the doctor's unreadiness for the weakening of the fabric between father and girl child. More particularly between father and girl child who had replaced the wife he never would have permitted to exist. I began to see not only the curb rein of her father but of her, in part, too willing submission — the malady and the sancrosanctness of their bond.

The move to Berkeley at first appeared like a liberation. Maxine, away from the watchful eye of her father and the years of forced dating with others, flourished in the stimulation of new books, new ideas, new modes of thinking. And with the flourishing, the love between her and Irwin grew in ardor and depth. And if the watchful collaborator within did not vanish with geographical distance, for part of the time at least its power was diminished.

During the spring semester her father suffered a heart attack, and in addition to the fear and pain of the attack itself, he suffered the fear and pain born of his professional knowledge. And with that fear, imperceptibly at first, he tightened the rein. On Maxine's return from her vigil at the hospital, she announced that she intended to dedicate her life to her father, his happiness and fulfillment. I remember that I demurred and I argued, but my words fell into some part of that ineffable distance that had marked our friendship from the outset. And as Maxine's mother hovered, nurse and wife in the hospital, in the home, so Maxine hovered from across the bay, an indistinct lover in the Berkeley hills, available and remote.

In our sophomore year, Maxine and I moved to our own apartment downhill and nearer the campus. Her mother, tacky in brown coat and lisle hose, supervised and helped us as we set up our own household. The doctor visited us at intervals, pale and domineering as an obituary. And Maxine gave him her thin bloodstream of love and, on the side, infrequently and with guilt, kept faith with Irwin.

For the last two years of college, Maxine and I lived separately. She moved to International House. I took an apartment with two new friends who, like me, were becoming involved with the social issues of the time. War loomed. Hitler was coming to power. We organized against fascism. We demonstrated for free speech. We called student strikes. Studying was sporadic and incidental. Maxine and I lunched together occasionally at an old haunt on Telegraph Avenue. She was working hard, going home weekends, trying not to see Irwin, seeing Irwin. We were awkward in the search for the old closeness. Still the caring. New distances. The need to translate.

The day of graduation, Maxine and I sat together on the stage at the Greek theatre; Irwin, with the students who were to receive their law degrees. Black caps and gowns, the hot annulling sun. My parents, Maxine's parents, Irwin's parents somewhere out there on the stone tiers. The long programs, tidy with the lists of graduates, of degrees and honors conferred.

It could not have been more than a week later that I received an excited and agitated call from Maxine. The day after the commencement ceremony, she reported, the doctor had called her into his study. "I see that your friend Irwin made Phi Beta Kappa and Law Review," he said, fingering the graduation program. And then in a tone almost of reproach, as if she had been withholding good news to which he was entitled, "Why didn't you tell me?" he asked. He insisted that she invite Irwin for dinner that Sunday. She said the warm candor of her father's manner and his assumption of what she thought she had kept well-hidden, their continued relation over the years, filled her old guilt with a new component of confusion.

After a jocular but stiff Sunday dinner, her father had summoned them both to his study, where her mother joined them. "I guess you two young schemers love each other," he said. Scarcely waiting for their affirmation, and in an act at once of encompassment and largesse, he secured their startled approval of an immediate marriage and determined that they should live in his house until Irwin was comfortably established in his profession.

If he had not anticipated Maxine's readiness for a boyfriend so many years earlier, he had now prematurely anticipated her readiness for a marriage he had gone to such lengths to prevent. Those tentative, permissible approaches and retreats, those encounters in freedom — in their circle at their time — to venture just far enough towards sex at their own pacing, all these had been denied them. Her voice on the phone sounded like that of the girl in the high school locker room.

It is curious that I have no memory of the wedding. Perhaps, feeling righteous in the freedom of the thirties, I felt some small contempt for those who had stayed within the strictures of class and convention. Perhaps it was the sudden, methodical haste of the marriage itself. The fact that I have little memory of the birth of her child I can more easily explain, for in my single state the world of children seemed a continent away. I do remember, however, her description of the birth and how her father, because he was a physician, admitted himself to the privacy of the labor room and supervised the delivery.

"Are you happy, now?" she asked me the afternoon of our last visit. By that time Irwin was a practicing attorney, and they were living in a flat of their own in the avenues and across the park from her parents. I was in graduate school in a desultory manner, very active in the antiwar movement of the campus and unhappy in some personal way that I can no longer recall. "I don't know," she said in response to the answer that I have fogotten, "when we were in high school and college and were depressed, we always thought everything would be all right if we could have the boyfriend we wanted. But here I am with a wonderful husband and a beautiful baby, and all I do is cry all day. And when Irwin comes home at night, I don't know why."

The distance from that quiet crying in the Sunset home to the gray tall building. The long ascent up the stairs and whatever time it took, and where she stopped to tear the labels from her clothes. The girl on the roof top. Did she hesitate before the steep fall to the pavement below?

And why had I not seen in that Berkeley visit the plumb-line of despair? What walled distanced protecting, obscuring?

The role of the witness unwitnessing. The gratuity of time. The paradox: so late the understanding. The diminishing of the seeming unalterable distance between the living and the dead. The dead girl freer in the living dream than the dreamer. The dream no longer returns. A final obeisance to a dead woman in the womb of a girl.

THE FOLLOWING WIND

Sneak time. Time as sneak, sneaking up on you, taking time away. Or to sneak time, take it for one's self away from everyone else. Like writing at night when he's asleep. Feeling sneaky. Or when the baby cries and they say, "Let him cry it out just two or three nights." But you don't and you won't and you sneak downstairs to the kitchen and sit, not in a rocker, but in a straight-backed chair, I don't know why, except all the comfort is between you and him, your body and his, so sensual, so comforting, your warm breasts and belly and his small accommodating belly and arms, the legs drawn up, the slightly acrid smell of urine in the diaper and the smell of milk from the bottle, not my breasts. They wouldn't let me nurse. In those days they said insufficient milk, elderly multipara. The medical insults. But I held him at night, and it was a secret from his father and his sisters and it was our secret and I have never told it before.

Chamber music. Not in my lady's chamber, but in the kitchen, which is not a chamber. He is my viola da gamba, my small cello, though I think of this only later when he takes up cello because the basses have not arrived at Interlochen. They question him because they say his parents are communist, which they are, but it has nothing to do with how he used to sing "And gathered the lambs to his bosom" and "Where'er you walk," which I taught him, and I think of it sometimes now, though he is a man, not only grown but even paunchy. Maybe it's our secret still, how I started listening to him sing and then went back to the world of poetry and music, saying not only what changes the world or what should be but also what is beautiful.

•

What I remember is that I was about nine or ten years old. We were in my aunt's studio, which was on the third floor of her home. My cousin Elizabeth, my sister Ethel and I. My aunt gave us each a box of pastels, and then, in the clear northern light of the room, she posed for us. Wearing a Japanese kimono in a rich, patterned brown, she sat in half profile, one wide sleeve draped over the arm of the small easy chair, the other folded under the elbow which rested on her lap. Her proper presence. The aquiline profile, its containment. The mouth with its intrinsic humor. The deep cleavage, which she seemed at once to display and to disregard. And all about us, her work: pastels of Golden Gate Park, green lawns and trees and small picnicking figures; still lifes, a vase with yellow chrysanthemums and wine-red tulips; portraits of friends and fellow-artists, of family. The walls covered with her framed pictures. Back to back against a desk, stacks of paintings in oil, in pastel.

My aunt's garden was the first place where I actually became acquainted with poetry, except for A Child's Garden of Verses, which was read to me when I was very small.

When I was sick, I was permitted to get into my mother's bed with the cool initialed linen sheets. I loved the sanction of Stevenson's poem about when he "was sick / And lay abed / And had [like me] two pillows at [his] head." I, too, had my toys all about me, though they were not soldiers on the counterpane. And I loved the sense of lift and motion in "O, how I love to go up in a swing / Up in the sky so blue." Recently I found myself reciting these lines to my grandson Pablo as I pushed him in the swing at Julius Kahn playground in the Presidio, timing each line to a push as he went higher and higher, and I looked at the blueness of the sky and the blue of his eyes. Later, I became enamored of Longfellow and mourned over the fate of Sir Federigo and the self-defeating sacrifice of his falcon for his lady love. Also I liked "The Children's Hour" for it's listing of "Grave Alice, and laughing Allegra, / And Edith with golden hair," wherein the reference to my name involved and honored me, though my hair was almost black with only occasional auburn lights in the bright sun. Much later, I read the epitaph Stevenson wrote for himself: "This be the verse you grave for me: / Here he lies where he longed to be; / Home is the sailor, home from sea; / And the hunter home from the hill."

I think I would like to collect epitaphs that writers have composed for themselves and study how diligently they refuse to relinquish control even in death. Yeats from the black headstone at Drumcliff: "Cast a cold eye / On death / Horseman pass by!" Jonathan Swift from the high catafalque in Saint Patrick's: "Here he lies — where savage indignation can lacerate his breast no more." Despite the note of self-pity, I am attracted to this one because even in the contemplation of death, Swift refuses to be complicitous with injustice or resigned to human cruelty.

It was in my aunt's garden as we sat in a circle and my aunt read to us that my cousin Matthew learned to recite "Sea Fever." In his short pants and his haircut with the bangs over his brow and his solemn face, he declaimed, ". . . all I ask is a merry yarn from a laughing fellow rover, / And quiet sleep and a sweet dream when the long trick's over." The poem made me think of the bay with the fish smell on the ferries when we went on outings to Berkeley, whitish grey seagull droppings, the groan of piles as the apron shoved against them, and foghorns blowing in the night.

•

When I was older, again in her garden, with the musky smell of marigolds in the air, we sat in the wooden garden chairs while our aunt introduced us to Wordsworth. I say *introduced* because the manner in which she presented him made for all the shyness, excitement, and anticipation of a personal encounter despite the fact that the presentation concerned only the poetry. It was approximately forty years later that I had another encounter with what seemed like the person of the poet himself, but this was in his own territory, in the Lake Country.

"The world is too much with us; late and soon!" my aunt recited. "Pretend," she said, "that there are two adjoining frames on the wall, each containing two pictures. The word *soon* is the left hand side of the first frame. 'Getting and spending, we lay waste our powers;' *powers* is a picture of you. 'Little we see in nature that is ours;' *ours* is a photograph of your sister. The next rhyme word, *boon* is the right side of the first frame. *Moon* is the left hand frame of the contiguous frame. *The winds* — we pronounce it wīnds in poetry," she said, "when we need to for the rhyme — 'that will be howling at all hours.' *Hours* is another picture of you." And so she continued throughout the octave, concluding with, "The first eight lines of the Italian sonnet are rhymed like this: frame picture picture frame frame picture picture frame."

My romance with the sonnets has continued until this day, but I have never grown to like the Lucy poems. There is something about the deliberate cultivation of simplicity that smacks of condescension. Coleridge remarked about "The Idiot Boy" that Wordsworth was the hero of his own work. That was after their collaboration on *The Preface to the Lyrical Ballads* and when they had come to a parting of the ways. On the other hand, I can see that it is a genuine gift to be simple and thereby to cut through the maze that obscures the sophisticated and egregious evil of the world.

•

There is a game I play with myself. I don't remember how it got started. I am driving in a car, and I see some obscure alley with, say, the name Shannon. I decide to commit to memory both the name and the location. In the game, someday someone will say, "I have a friend who lives on a little one-block street by the name of Shannon." And I will say, "Oh sure. I know that street. It runs for one block between Van Ness and Polk and McAllister and Golden Gate." The reason I am so impressed with my own role is that I am in reality singularly oblivious to names and locations of streets and avenues. The only hitches in my game are that no one ever asks me about a friend living on

Shannon Street, and that if anyone did, I would have forgotten both the name and the location.

Then there are the insomnia games. Name a woman poet for every letter in the alphabet: Akhmatova, Elizabeth Barrett Browning, Lucille Clifton, Dickinson, of course, (I'm stuck on *E*. I'll come back to it), Forché, Giovanni. (Stuck again.) Try breeds of dogs: airedale, boxer, collie, Dalmatian, English setter, fox terrier, Gordon setter, harrier (Are they a breed? Yeats said, "She rode to harriers."), Irish setter. (I'm stuck on *J*.) Go back to poets. By this time, either I have fallen asleep or am wide awake fixating on finding a poet *E* or a dog *J*.

From these paste-ups I construct my days and nights. But of course that's an untruth. My life is largely constructed of more mundane but self-respecting pursuits. I rise in the morning when nobody else is awake. Usually I do a wash. There is something very self-organizing about laundry. When the spin cycle is finished, I put the wash in the dryer, being careful to pull out the cottons before they shrink. Then I bring coffee and the newspaper to Dave. Since his legs have been giving him trouble, I like him to stay in bed as long as he can in the morning. Fortunately his work is such that he can do most of it over the phone without getting up. Next I pick up the house. This is harder than it sounds because mornings I have an agenda of worries which keeps me in a state of levitation and to pick up a room you need to descend systematically to every surface. I put dishes from my midnight foraging into the dishwasher, tidy the sponges on the sink, notice the yellow one is falling apart. They have been wearing out more rapidly since I read an article on the danger of salmonella bacteria retained on sinks and in sponges and have been soaking them weekly in a strong clorox solution. The proportions, according to the article, need only be one to eight, but I don't like the smell to get in a measuring cup, so I guess the proportions and no doubt err on the side of strength, to which my malodorous hands for the remainder of the day well attest. From the sink I go to the stove and see the grease spattered from last night's lamb chops. I scrub it with the shabby sponge and then observe the collection of grease or dirt wedged between the stove and the tile surface adjoining it but with a crack just large enough for soil to enter. I take a dull knife and, holding it upside down, force the dirt to the surface. Actually it's quite gratifying, seeing a narrow peel of black grease emerge. Like getting hair and phlegm out of the bathtub trap with a tweezer. You start pinching what you think is a little knot of hair, and lo and behold, a large repulsive accumulation of mucous and hair emerges like some garden slug.

But back to the kitchen. I haven't even gotten to the table or the surface on the far side of the sink with its assortment of ball point pens with lost or unfitting tops, my extra glasses, a grocery list from yesterday, two clips, a stamp, a blue pad with two phone numbers for Dave. When I think I'm all through, I say to myself, "Look carefully at *every* surface," and there's always something I've missed when I was levitating about bathroom traps or less manageable worries such as my mother's health and care and Dave's legs and whether I should wait for my teenage grandchildren to come back, so to speak, or whether I should pursue them. I've written elsewhere about the dreadful democracy of lists, how everything becomes flattened and equalized: the headlines threatening war in the Persian Gulf and the need for a new washer in the faucet. You notice I have not mentioned myself among my anxieties, my worry that I am not writing, the fact that "at my back I always hear," etc.

•

The problem is that writing erases memory the way you erase a tape by talking over it. I guess that serves a purpose if the memory is disagreeable and one wants to lay it to rest. But it is also a kind of leeching: the blood goes into the leech and one's history into squiggles on the lines of a yellow pad. When the memory is pleasant or even neutral, it's like cutting the string of a kite and watching it soar erratically into the windy welkin or plunge and flatten on the Marina Green.

When I was nine and a half and my sister was twelve, she would chase me around the house, up and down the stairs, taunting: "I have a little sister and she has no breasts." (Running up the stairs to the first landing), "What will we do with my sister in the day when she will be spoken for?" (Chasing me down the back stairway), "I am a wall but my breasts are like towers." Each night when I was in the bath, I called my mother. "Mother, Mother, have I started to develop?" I asked, and every night, feeling the flat nipples, she would say, "Not yet," until the night the slight tender swelling began.

•

Troilus standing on the towered wall looked down upon the plain and waited for Criseyde to return, but when it became clear that she was not going to, he went home to Troy. "Despair for the son of Priam / Was a high-walled town. / High towers and shining turrets / And terror when you looked down."

And I too, only in reversal, I a woman in a hotel room on the fourteenth floor, waiting. I thought perhaps he had the hotel wrong or the wrong date, but I knew he didn't, and I became an emptiness and I vacated my body. I grew so thin my figure was beautiful, my head perched like a bird on the deserted body, and the windows drew me to them. But I was not a bird, and I knew I did not want to die. Then I went to the youth parliament, and I delivered a fiery speech against war, and the windy vacancy in my head swirled out words, strong words, while my body was all tremor. When I returned home from Los Angeles, my mother said, "I have never interfered, but I am interfering now. See what is happening to you." So I went to my aunt's house and sat in the third floor studio. The photographer placed a striped cloth behind me as a background. Her name was Sonia Noskowiak. She had worked with Weston. I wanted to record that I had been young and perhaps at one time beautiful.

•

"It was very hard on Mr. and Mrs. Wordsworth those last years when Dorothy was quite out of her mind," said the caretaker as she showed us Wordsworth's study. She spoke as if the Wordsworths had left only last month. Dove Cottage, set in the ebullient greenness of the Lake Country, seemed meager and ascetic, and the caretaker herself, with her gray hair and drab cardigan, seemed as plain as the cottage. I tried to imagine the poet at his desk or rummaging in the small bookcase, and I tried to see him lying on the couch, "in vacant or in pensive mood," recapturing the elation he had experienced on seeing a field of daffodils. But it was not until I myself had seen a field of daffodils that I could really understand. More recently, in reading Dorothy's journals, I found myself resenting how her brother had used her observations as he had in many ways used her. I found myself resenting the self-congratulatory observation of his own transport, and I understood how Dorothy, who cradled her "dear William's head" on her lap and who accompanied him on his honeymoon, might indeed go "quite out of her mind."

•

Maybe it happened because Honor had turned to me in the intermission of the Saturday workshop and asked, "Do you know the poem?" For whatever reason, the lines came to me during dinner tonight, and I tried to recite them to Dave, but I could get only as far as "Earth, receive an honored guest," and I began to cry. Dave said, "Go on. Say it." So I stood behind him and put my lips against his head and said: "Earth, receive an honored guest; / William Yeats is laid to rest: / Let the Irish vessel lie / Emptied of its poetry."

What has been happening, I think, is that there has been a kind of cresting lately. Like a wave about to break. My life feels full alternately of poetry and despair. I look about and tell myself how lucky I am, but the very richness fills me with fear of loss.

•

Matthew and I had been close as children. When we were very small, I initiated a flying club. Our arms flapping like wings, we ran down the street, convinced that we were airborne. Later, we each had an Irish setter puppy, which we got from the Colbert Kennels in South San Francisco.

Matthew chose a male, all camel-colored the way Irish setter pups are before they become lanky and turn a glorious auburn. I chose an older female, sweet and sensitive and friendly and already copper-toned.

I always wondered whether Matthew cried when his dog died. I cried until my eyes were swollen shut and my nose was so stuffed up I couldn't breathe. When I stopped crying, I ran down the brick stairs to the ivy-colored turn where the mailbox was. Mr. Villapando was just coming into the entrance. His long mustachios curving upward, his shoulders rounded into the perpetual posture of the cellist, he encompassed me with his arms, and with his hands against the wall pinned me so there was no escape. "Little girl, little girl," he said in his thick Castilian accent, his breath in my face, the smell of his tweed jacket heavy between us, his warm concern making me feel even lonelier in my grief, "What is the matter?" Mr. Villapando was Ethel's cello teacher. Every morning she practiced — the long, lugubrious bowstrokes indistinguishable from the adenoidal sound of foghorns in the bay.

My setter died in the midst of a distemper epidemic. Each night I prayed for all the dogs who were dead. "Dear God," I intoned, "please bless Lassie and Butch and Jackie and Trump," the list nightly getting longer and longer. Then there was the list of living dogs whose welfare depended upon my intervention. After the dogs came all my relatives and friends, all waiting upon my protection.

When the responsibility grew too heavy, I dispensed with God. Not in a profound wrestling with myself or with His representative. It happened in a kind of epiphany one day when I was sitting on the toilet. Suddenly I realized I no longer believed, and my reverence was unceremoniously and quite finally flushed down the drain.

•

"Fall on you knees / Oh hear the angel voices," Dayani sang in her rich alto voice, her long copper braids dangling to her waist, her Irish setter eyes rapt and staring, her prognathous jaw struck forward in mock piety as she allowed herself to fall to the ground. We were misfits, she and I, in a girls' camp in the Sierra, Dayani sent away by her Indian father and her rich English mother who toured the concert stage in a sari and sang in wealthy drawing rooms like those of Catherine's parents where the grownups exchanged knowing looks, spoke of her as an animus-ridden woman, and punned upon her professional name, Ratan Devi, saying she certainly was rotten. Catherine, too, had been a misfit in the jolly sportsmanship atmosphere of Huntington Lake Camp for Girls. Catherine taught us "A maiden fair to see / The pride of minstrelsy" from *Pinafore* and Amiens sad song from *As You Like It.* "Blow, blow, thou winter wind! / Thou art not so unkind As man's ingratitude" and the spiritual in which each stanza ends with the refrain, "There's no hiding place down there."

•

Fifty years and I have not forgotten: Dayani of the Irish setter eyes and the auburn hair. When you visited us thirty years ago, your hair was short and lustreless, a sad maiden lady, we thought. You told us you had been studying with Casals in Prades. "The lessons were very expensive," you said, and then with the old controlled irony, "I could never have afforded them save for a wealthy lover." And Catherine on that great Peninsula estate, surrounded with books and music and servants and adults who made annual pilgrimages to Zurich to study with Jung, Catherine with your gold diaphanous hair surrounding your tall brow ("She looks like Joan of Arc seeing a vision," her sister said). How the adults surrounded you with protection, living as they did in fear of the demons in your genes, and how only a few years later those demons occupied that lofty brow so that you lived out your life in a sanitarium, nurtured and protected in a cottage of your own by your childhood nurse. "Blow, blow, thou winter wind! / Thou art not so unkind / . . . As friend remembered not." I do not forget you, lost women of my youth.

And then, in the midst of it, a terrible confusion: whether it is exploitation of the dead to accommodate them to the theater of my mind, where they remain alive as their deaths splinter into new meanings. Maxine, for example, and how at last she freed herself from her father. How she stood on the roof of the tallest building, how she tore the Macy's label from her coat, the Livingston label from her dress, her poor identities, and how she jumped and fell. And I know now she did not want to die. But her father had chosen her, would not let her go though she had left him for husband and baby. And the fall broke the long leash so that for one moment, until she struck the pavement, her body buffeted by winds between the high buildings, she was, she thought, free. And whether this is my story, though hers, and the confusion in the telling.

•

The first setter was succeeded by an eighteen-month-old bitch, past the age of distemper and crowned with an illustrious name and pedigree. June of Conarhu, however, never lived up to her ancestry or the grandeur of her name. Her ears were not quite long enough, her coat not sufficiently burnished, with always some lighter hairs showing through the copper glow. Every year I exhibited her in the American Kennel Club competition. "Show, June," I would say as the dogs were displayed in a circle of tanbark around the presiding judge; "Show, June," again because she seemed in the rink to forget our long training sessions and turned her body in a loop so that her nose came around to where I held her tail. Then I would hold the rectangular head forward with my left hand and kneeling on the tanbark, place her in the show position, front paws parallel and close, one back leg forward, the other extended.

I loved the atmosphere of the dog show, the professional talk among the exhibitors, the smells of dogs and sawdust, the rows and rows of stalls with their different breeds — short-haired wirehaired fox terriers, Boston bulls, Great Danes, the black and brown Gordon setters, that mysterious restored breed the Irish wolfhound, its stupid inbred cousin the Russian wolfhound, the mosquito-like Mexican hairless, and the wheezing underslung Pekingese, the beautiful lean, spotted Dalmations, and the elegant Afghan hounds, the dachshunds long-haired and short. I loved the intense, parochial, carnival atmosphere and the dog-breeders who would treat me as one of their own.

•

To lock in. To lock out. Lockets with someone's hair. Looking like spun gold and a brooch to match. They were Ethel's. But the brooch can be a locket on a chain around my neck. Mother wore a locket with Ethel's picture in it after Ethel's death. She lost it when she was downtown getting a hairdo. When she found it was missing, she put an ad in the paper and someone answered it. A cruel gag.

"If you tell me how to breathe, I won't choke," I said. The doctor didn't pay any attention. He had a large instrument down my throat. The nurse said, "Breathe through your nose even if it is hard." I thought it's like natural childbirth. Concentrate on breathing. When I was in labor for the third time, it seemed as if I had been in it continuously with nothing in between. It's the same way in the dentist chair. Periods of intense concentration and intense dissociation. And besides that, the strange postures and all that machinery and metal and stirrups and scopes. A sense of time having come to a halt, a clock that has wound down. Then the new baby in my arms and the body feeling utterly clean and pure. Like being in love for the first time.

Once downtown with Rachel and she in her early womanhood, I saw our reflections in a store window and mistook her for me. Now it is true others have always seen a strong resemblance, but I had never seen it before.

I met Mr. Berg on Cole Street. "Everything's wonderful when you are in love," he said, looking silly. Narcissus at seventy looks in the stream and sees himself at twenty. "I would that my love would silently flow / Like a single word." Mendelssohn, I'm certain, but I am not certain of the last two words. Anyway, it's a translation.

I can't sing anymore. A range of only five notes. Therefore I can't take down themes in *solfège*. Ethel and I took a class in ear training from Ernest Bloch at the Conservatory. When we first heard *Threepenny Opera,* we took down the "Beggars' March" in *solfège*. That was 1930 in Carmel. Pre-

Blitzstein. His awful death in a bar. Some homophobe. The body is so tidy until it spills. Blood, I mean. The other liquids have their own locks and dams.

My friend said that when she was a child she wondered why they had *lox* in the Panama Canal. The Jewish children were told we should be quiet on streetcars because Jews were supposed to be noisy. And don't gesture with your hands or use Jewish expressions like schliemiel. We never discussed money. At Sunday school we learned the "Ode to Joy" with the words "Onward, brothers, march still onward / Side by side and hand in hand. / We are bound for man's true kingdom. / We will reach the promised land."

Swan's Oyster House delivered oysters on the half-shell in their own beds of salted ice. For fancy dinner parties. My mother entertained Ernest Bloch, who spent the whole evening talking about his feet. He had just composed a national anthem: "America, America, your song is in my heart." Everyone knew it was dreadful. The ladies who ran the Conservatory brought him. They thought he was perfect. People called them the Vestal Virgins. Ethel and I were allowed to sit on the stairs while the grownups were having dinner. How strange their talk and the sudden rise of their laughter. We clutched our nightgowns tight around our legs lest one of them come up the stairs to visit with us.

At Point Lobos in the tide pools, starfish and sea anemone. The sea anemone open and close like vaginas. The thick lips. We were all having affairs. It was vacation. From college. From the student movement. She lived in Carmel. Her name was Winter. She was older than we were. When she stole our boyfriends, I said, "If Winter comes . . . ." Her husband was very old. "Age cannot wither . . . ." But it can. Look at Elizabeth Taylor. Yeats knew. Twice I spent hours looking through his *Collected Works* to find where he had rhymed "rage" and "age." I don't know why I didn't write it down the first time and save myself trouble.

On the other hand, and for no apparent reason, some lines stick in memory. For example: "Yea, though the jesses were my dear heartstrings . . . ;" the next line is "I'ld whistle her off." To be able to let go. To learn to care and not to care. I said, "It's because hair is very important to women." That's when she felt very bad about the prospect of losing it, and they said to buy a wig before it came out and besides it would come back. "I hope so," she said. The trouble is that you can use very poor judgement as to when to let go. Look at Othello. The choice isn't usually that dramatic. I'm talking about how long one can hold on to the hand of a drowning person and not drown. To be there to hold that hand until the very last moment.

When Davy was eleven, he was in the Boys' Chorus. One Sunday they were invited to a black church where they sang "Jesus walked that lonesome valley." Davy had been in a fight and had a real shiner. Nevertheless, he looked very spiritual in the white robe. I've thought a lot about the next line, "You have to walk it by yourself."

Honor said, "Remembered poetry serves to stop the flow of time for you. It allows you to be still."

•

Iphigenia knew there was no wind in the tall sails but she pleaded, she said, "Father, why must you? I do not want to die. Why must you?" And the wind rose and the sails filled like bellies of pregnant women, and it was all about two sisters, the beautiful one and the one left be-

116

hind, her daughter dead, her husband all wind and heroism, a murderer, and then the long war.

Sara Bard Field told me that during World War I she became sick and delirious and in her delirium heard marching feet of all the dead soldiers. So upon her recovery she wrote the poem "We Whom the Dead Have Not Forgiven." This was some years before her own son was killed in an automobile accident, she having been at the wheel. She wrote: "We whom The Dead have not forgiven / Must hear forever the ominous beat, / For the free, light, rippled air of heaven / Is burdened now with dead men's feet . . . ."

"Although it sounds self-serving, our children," Dave said, "are the only immortality we know."

•

When we were staying with John and Rachel, John and I went for a walk. We started out through the green meadow behind their house, past the high school track, went through a path that came out on the dirt road by the cemetery. I have always disliked cemeteries, having known only the ones on the outskirts of San Francisco, with their rows and rows of anonymous dead from the wars or the formal, obsequious ones where the wealthy are buried below overtended gardens or their ashes stored in urns, stacked in catacombs, pretentious and cold. But this New England cemetery is entirely different. To lie in a grave on a green hillside, where grass grows freely and a white stone marks one's grave. To lie near the house where one has lived and where one's family still lives, so that death becomes not an obscene mockery of life but its quiet continuance — here death is domesticated.

As we walked, the moist grasses pricked our ankles, and because we walked at an angle across the field, we could look back at the old red house and see Rachel hanging laundry on the parallel clothes lines, Anya running through the sprinkler.

John is my son-in-law. He is a quiet man, and it has always seemed a generosity that on these walks he lifts his silence and talks of his life, of his folks who have farmed this land since early colonial days, his love for Rachel, his pride in her and Anya and now the little one, Rosie, who rides this afternoon in a blue canvas pack on his back.

Today Rosie is wide awake, although yesterday on Rachel's back when we walked through town she seemed lulled to sleep by the motion. I wonder what it is to her to take in the broad expanse of meadow, the cows grazing, their full brown udders taut, two horses grazing, a white and a bay, their soft nostrils nuzzling the grass. The sweet smell of the meadow. Or when we emerge at the far end of the open space and walk single file through a path so overgrown her father has to push the heavy branches aside and hold them back, and she must smell their heavy mustiness. It's possible that I would not remember this particular walk, not distinguished from the walks we take each spring, had it not been for the horses.

As we emerge on the dusty country road, a car rushes by so that John and I, who had been walking abreast, again go single file. I notice the breeze pushing Rosie's white cotton bonnet back from her head and the ties growing tight around her neck, but not so tight as to bother her, I observe her feet splayed outwards resting on the wooden bar of the backpack. I think of how she turns her head to watch the car. I was never so conscious or so curious with my own children of the catalogue of experiences they process the first two years, how the hands explore space, the head learns the motions of assent and denial, and all the rich certitude of language to assert, repel, control comes to their disposal along with the seductions of pretend and play.

A half mile down the dirt road, a parade of cars, their headlights shining, came towards us. John said, "It's probably someone from the town. So few of us live here, I always feel as if I should know the dead and be participating in the funeral." Then John asked me about my life in San Francisco, and I told him about my book and the gratification of seeing it in print after all the private years. I asked him about his practice, and he told me he liked working with individual patients and not with institutions and then that he had some paper work to do and we had better be heading home.

We turned around and started to walk back. Just as we arrived at the juncture where we would leave the dirt road for the path leading to the cemetery, we heard three loud shots. I was alarmed at the closeness of gunfire, thinking we might be in the path of hunters, but John assured me that no one would be hunting there and that the shots were ceremonial ones that accompany a military funeral. No sooner had he finished than we heard a bugle sounding taps. Then suddenly there was a pounding of hooves, and the two horses, white and bay, galloped by us in fright, their tangled manes by force of wind aslant from their extended necks.

•

Sunday morning at the Caffé Roma. It's like church for us. Starts the day off. Sunday friends we meet there each week. No common denominator but the caffé with its ceilings of angels and cherubim, its bright white cappuccino or the tall pale latte. We borrow chairs from the adjoining tables and crowd together, knees touching, chairs angled to make more room, Sunday papers sprawled amid the cups.

Howie, the writer, joins us. Michael, the seaman painter, shows us two still lifes. They are small watercolors of flowers and fruit. "Which do you want?" he asks. I reflect for a moment and say, "The one with the purple background." But he says, "Take both." Leslie is seven; she is my granddaughter. Her favorite color is purple, so I got her a purple dress for her birthday. It is too long, but her mother won't shorten it because she says it makes her look like Jo in *Little Women*. Today she wears it as she meets us at the caffé with her mother. She likes to walk up the block to the Italian bakery with Dave. On the way there, Dave holds her right hand in his left and holds his cane in the other. Leslie adjusts her pace to his and takes three carefully spaced steps to his two. On the way back, Leslie is holding a bag of cookies. She shows me the pink gingerbread man and the green star with crystallized sugar decorations. She has taken a bite out of each.

I was slow in embracing the estate of grandmotherhood because I was just getting through with mothering when the first grandchild came along. Nevertheless I have a special feeling for that grandchild and last summer wrote him a letter in the form of a poem. It was on the occasion of his volunteering for a reforestation program in Nicaragua. I did not send it and will not show it to him until he is through with all his teenage crazies, which the poem enumerates before saying my love for him has been a secret scolding in the heart.

This day in the Roma, Anya sits on my lap. They are visiting us from the East. Anya is very quiet. When her mouth is in repose, the deep indentation in her upper lip is that of my family — my father in his early manhood, so prim and sensitive and righteous in the brown photograph — my mouth and my son's as well.

I say to Howie, "There's a story for you: those two beautiful young sisters at the table behind us." I can tell they are sisters by the sharp identical cut of their nostrils and the soft revelatory lips, though the mouth of the older one begins to take the shape of her separate life. Howie has been on a creative binge. He has written thirty-six stories in three months. He credits me as a catalyst because I asked him one day why he was not writing from the free and affective side of his nature. I have not been writing at all. "Physician, heal thyself," I think ruefully. Now I say to him, "Henry James says a writer is one on whom no experience is lost." On the spot he writes a story incorporating me, Henry James, the two sisters, and his immediate compelling attraction to the older one. He does not name the attraction, but he conveys it by describing a sensual gesture she made to scoop up some salt her sister had spilled.

I want to write my own story about them. In it I would notice them as they meet at the caffé. They have not seen each other for some months, or perhaps they have, but it has not been on neutral turf. I would describe the way their mouths curl and the flight of their eyebrows. I think they have been independent of their family for a long time, though the older one is only in her early twenties and the younger in her late teens. Suddenly I realize that I shall never know their real story.

Once on a train from Baja — and even then I did not know the name of the station where we stopped — I saw a small boy mount the steps of a railway carriage. It must have been fifty years ago, so that small boy if he is still living is now a grizzled man and probably remembers the parting as a beginning of sorts. He was wearing a gray wool suit, home-tailored, with its calf-length knickers meeting gray socks that rested in black foreign shoes. The man and woman who were seeing him off looked too old to be his parents. They had the sorrowful, resigned faces of the exile. Where was he going? Who would meet him? Forlorn small expatriate in the European clothes, where were you going?

Or Juan Vallejo, newsboy in Mexico City. You got in trouble with the professional guides when you offered to show us around. Where is your hero now, the wrestler Gorilla Masyas? Did you become a wrestler, too? Where are you now?

I wanted to invent a life for the two sisters so that I would not lose them. But they are recalcitrant strangers — discrete, possessive, solipsist, enclosed as a line drawing.

HOSPITAL PIECE

Midnight. I cannot sleep. I have been here since noon. Monitored. My heart recorded in a foreign language on a screen above my head. Invaded with needles. Blood pressure taken hourly. Lines of poetry come at me. Disjunctive, no doubt misremembered. Lines about the heart. Heart as metaphor. The unreliability of the heart. "My heart being hungry feeds on food / The fat of heart despise" . . . and . . . "while my bitter heart observes the truth / My mind spoke false, 'You cannot hurt me now.' " But none about that prosaic, vulnerable mechanism wanting oxygen within the cage of my ribs. Then the one that haunts me though I know I am pre-empting it for a meaning far from its own . . . "thou wouldst not think how ill all's here about my heart."

Prodigious night mounted in aloneness where I can reach for no one.

A night of prodigies. Yehudi in his velvet Little Lord Fauntleroy suit with the lace collar, his aquiline face with the slender, curving nostrils, the violin clutched hard against the silk handkerchief protecting his chin, the high exalted brow. Isaac Stern in the living room of the Koshland house two blocks behind the hospital where I now lie, his tailor father proudly beside him. Hilda Conkling dictating her poems to her mother, her child face on the fly leaf of her book. Nathalia Crane, poor distorted nightingale, "In the darkness who would cavil o'er the question of a line / Since the darkness holds all loveliness, beyond the mere design."

I walk the hospital corridor with the nurse where at the far west end I can see through the window the corner of Cherry and Clay the grey shingled house where I was born. My mother said that when they brought me to her all the lashes were turned under the lids of my eyes, and she told me how she carefully, gently worked them out. I think of her now, so old and frail, lying in her home, and here am I in a hospital two blocks from my beginnings, my chest crunched with pain, worrying about the pain my being here will bring her as my birth itself had done. "All things return upon themselves / mother to child and child again to her / all things return . . . clocked in the anarchy of time I turn, / turn and return at once mother and child / shore to your lake, mother to steepening pole / All things return."

•

This morning by King Ambulance to another hospital where the angioplasty will be done. Down Sacramento Street, past the corner store where we bought Nu-Chus after school, the sweet chocolate, the chewy aromatic white inside. You would bite in and pull the bar away from your teeth, the white rubbery middle that would not give so its strings went from your mouth to your hand where the chocolate was melting along your fingers. My cousin, Elizabeth, ate a Nu-Chu and a pickle, and I said, "Elizabeth, how could you?" We drive past Loustau's French laundry still where it was, but now the new expanse of doctors' offices, expensive shops for antiques, children's toys, shoe stores closing out daily. I took Leslie to Dottie Doolittle's before her birthday, pretending I wanted her to help choose a dress for another child. Then I went back without her and got the purple dress she liked. A year later before Miranda's wedding, I took Leslie to the Junior Boot Shop a block away, where I had taken her mother some forty years ago.

The paramedic who is sitting with me in the ambulance is an olive-skinned Italian-American whose family came from Sicily. He is very kind, chatty, nonintrusive. We talk about my childhood in this neighborhood and his in North Beach.

•

I am now at Pacific Medical Center — an I.V. in my left arm, three monitor pads on my chest, a nitro-paste patch above my left breast, my stomach full of valium, tylenol. Two Filipino technicians come in to prep me for the needles that will be inserted in my groin. I ask, "Are you going to give me a pubic Mohawk?" but they pay no attention. They wear his and her shower caps, latex gloves. They are quiet and detached and I feel as if I am being prepared by undertakers. I had read a story in *Granta* yesterday about a part-time undertaker who kept coffins stacked in his basement and how various family members would sleep in them at different times. Edith Sitwell, I remember, would lie in her coffin daily for a spell before starting to write.

I am in the wings of the jump where fear abides on hold. At the Saint Francis Riding Academy, I try to hold back the big bay gelding, struggling with his mouth as he skids at a canter around the corner of the ring, I pulling hard on the snaffle until we are into the whitewashed wings. Then standing in the short stirrups, feet pushed in so that the metal lies between my arch and the heel of the brown riding boots, I let him go. No way back for me now, the heavy horse must gauge for himself how many strides he needs before he elevates, pushed by the muscular withers. If he gauges wrong, he may stop suddenly, swerve, propel me over his head so I fall, perhaps one foot briefly caught in the stirrup, and land on the tanbark. Or he is over the jump. Then the rush of triumph, the adrenalin still in the veins. But here no triumph. Over the jump, so-to-speak, and the heart can breathe again or else.

The night nurse told me his favorite poet was Yeats and his favorite poem, "The Wild Swans at Coole." I asked him whether he knew the poem "On a Political Prisoner" because during the day I was looking at the doves outside my window on the sill. At first I had seen their heads only and mistaken them for rats, but when I saw they were birds, I thought of the poem Yeats had written about Countess Markiewicz, "She that but little patience knew / From childhood on / Had now so much / A grey gull lost its fear and flew / Down to her cell and there alit, / And there endured her fingers' touch . . . " I thought I too must learn her patience and gentleness. The next morning when I sat up in bed, I could see the whole window sill was encrusted with bird droppings, and I wanted rid of their jerking heads and endless monotonous cooing.

•

Once long ago when I was in a hospital awaiting surgery, I left Dave a poem. It was Emily Dickinson's, but he thought it was mine. It read: "My period had come for Prayer / No other Art would do — / My tactics lacked a rudiment — Creator — Was it you?" When Davy was in a motor scooter accident and lay unconscious in Mills Memorial Hospital in San Mateo, Rachel said she wished she could pray as I wish I could now.

I am being wheeled to the cath lab. I am being exceedingly clever. The way I used to be with the unbearable bourgeois boys when I was a young girl and then would wonder why I sat, a melancholy wallflower, at the German-Jewish dances where you wore a white gardenia on your left shoulder and it was crushed brown by your reluctant partner whose hair smelled of pomade and who hated clever girls who did not know how to play cute. So on the gurney I say, "This is my third time round. I guess I'm a recidivist," and they say, "Lie perfectly still and we will move you to the table." By this time the tranqs have worked and anyway I am in the wings of the jump. First they put the needle and then the long tube in my right groin. I see it on the screen move up the artery to the swimming grey and white that is my heart. I become an interested stranger in a dark theater, as they say, "Take a deep breath and hold" and move the camera and say, "Take a deep breath and hold," and it's all so impersonal, someone lying there surrounded by green gowns and shower caps and doctors wearing glasses with side windows, all very kind and distant, and I am theirs and I am absent though willingly here and they say, "Ah, there is the blockage."

•

She thought it should be pink or yellow and should ascend the artery, wafting like a birthday balloon as it leaves Anya's hand or it should rise, rise into the sky the way the balloons soar into the firmament at the end of the opera in the park when they let them loose after everyone sings the drinking song from *La Traviata*, but when she asked to see the balloon before they inserted it in the groin, it was a small plastic object, like a tiny condom, on the end of a tubing. As it reached the blockage in the artery, they expanded it so the pressure in her chest was a possessing and the rest of the body became an appendage. And this time they held it longer than they had in the previous procedures and then released, and they expanded the artery ten times and then released and they speculated whether to expand it wider or whether that would explode the passage and they decided not to. Then they said, "That is all," and "You did fine." Someone patted her on the shoulder and said, "We'll take you back to your room. Ease yourself on to the gurney without moving your right leg. A little more. That's good." At first they couldn't find her husband where he was waiting, but soon he came into her room looking supportive and scared. Then the doctor came in and said the procedure had gone well, and they put a nitroplast between her breasts and the plastic was stiff and stuck into her left breast. So she descended back into her body.

She had to lie absolutely still and inert for forty-eight hours and her body was not her own but a province ruled by physicians and nurses and lab technicians with their batteries of needles and tubes. For the first twenty-four hours, they kept a five pound sand pack on the groin, and even after that they said, "Do not move your leg at all," and they took over like an occupying army.

•

I brought my body to the hospital, but I left without it. No, I brought my self to the hospital but left without it.

There are ten marks where the EKG terminals have been. There is a purple bruise where the heparin lock has been. Bruise on my left hand where they couldn't get the needle in. Bruise where the I.V. entered. Bruises where they took blood. Bruise in my groin where the tube had entered.

Any way you look at it a division of the self. Don't tell me you can't separate psyche and soma. Mine are not only separated but divorced. Home from the hospital yesterday, and it was either psyche or soma that came up the stairs acting pale but as if nothing had happened. Then the indeterminate dyad, the eternal busybody tried to get them together. Or is the indeterminate dyad the *I* who sat us all down and tried to talk it out until I blew an anginal fuse.

•

The trouble with feeling well again is that it is so dangerous. Any moment it can be taken away. For example, afterwards I sit in the garden in the old redwood chair with the new blue cushions I had bought so the garden would look nice for Miranda's wedding. Richard had planted

some red salpaglossa on the first level and where the ter-
race began, some tall, red linaria. Up the lattice describing
the south boundary of the garden, a small vine creeps en-
tangling itself with the wooden network. And because I
feel calm and happy and the benign autumn smell of the
garden monitors my breathing, I feel nothing can be
wrong.

But then I know it is not true and that the clock in the
belly of the alligator is ticking with no relation to what I am
thinking or feeling and all is aleatory, disjunctive and the
mind, a humming bird with a thousand inperceptible wing
strokes as it poises against the rose which blossoms its last
shining pink and below it the serrated leaves. ("O ROSE,
thou art sick / The invisible worm / . . . Does thy life
destroy.")

•

I have spent three months trying to reconcile myself to
the treachery of my heart. In an Emily Dickinson poem,
there is an opening line, "Renunciation is a piercing virtue
— / The letting go / A presence — for an Expectation . . . "
I tried substituting "Resignation" for "Renunciation," but
it does not work because resignation is a train stopped or
moving backwards on a track. I have no expectation of an
afterlife wherein I can look down on Anya and Rosie as
their breasts ripen, on Leslie when she turns from her Bar-
bie dolls, or Pablo when his boy energy takes off in who
knows what direction.

Jan Kott, with scorn, disposes of the Aristotelian defini-
tion of tragedy. He says that the central theme of the tragic
is that man is sentient and yet must die. The problem for

me is with the mechanism of the final curtain: how to enjoy what transpires on stage when you are waiting for the curtain to descend, not when you think it is supposed to, but whenever its faulty mechanism lets go.

•

"My heart ever faithful / Sings praises to God be joyful." I did not know what this aria was from. Caryl ran it down and says it is actually a cantata by that name. Why do these lines haunt me, being so far from the framework of my belief and so deriding in the false promise of comfort? Once I asked students in a midterm to paraphrase Hopkins' sonnet "No worst. There is none." One student paraphrased the line, "Comforter, where is thy comforting" as "Quilt where is thy warmth." Maybe that is a perfectly adequate agnostic equivalent.

NOTES

Page 22.   "Oppie"
J. Robert Oppenheimer was a physicist on the faculty of the University of California at Berkeley. Later he was the director of the atomic energy research project at Los Alamos from 1942 to 1945 and was instrumental in the development of the atomic bomb.

Page 23.   "Loyalist Spain"
In 1936 a Popular Front government consisting of republicans, socialists, communists, and syndicalists was victorious in elections. A rebellion led by Francisco Franco and supported by Hitler and Mussolini waged a civil war against the government. The defense of the government forces known as Loyalist became a cause célèbre among intellectuals, liberals, and radicals.

Page 27.   "Moscow trials"
Stalin instigated a series of show trials against many of the old Bolsheviks alleging they were involved in Trotskyist plots. There were thousands of victims of what were known as the purges.

Page 34.   "Krushchev report"
In 1956 Krushchev reported to the Twentieth All-Union Party Congress of the USSR and revealed the full extent of Stalin's crimes.

Page 37.   "AEC Personal Security Board"
            When Oppenheimer opposed the decision to build a
            hydrogen bomb, the Atomic Energy Commission sus-
            pended his clearance for access to classified data. After
            hearings before the AEC's Personnel Security Board in
            the Spring of 1954, the AEC confirmed the recommen-
            dation of the Board that his clearance not be renewed.

WITH STONES FROM THE GORGE

Page 41.   "The committee"
            The Burns Committee was a California Senate fact-
            finding committee set up to investigate ostensibly sub-
            versive activities. It was the successor of the Yorty and
            Tenney committees that had conducted investigations
            of Hollywood, of teachers' involvement in the Ameri-
            can Federation of Teachers in Los Angeles, and of the
            Rad lab in Berkeley. It investigated, among other
            things, the university campuses and the peace move-
            ment. The particular hearing mentioned in this piece
            occurred in 1951.

Page 45.   "The False Armistice"
            In World War I, shortly before the Armistice of Novem-
            ber 11, 1918, the newspapers fallaciously reported an
            armistice that became the occasion for great rejoicing,
            followed by enormous disappointment.

Page 51–   "Strikers' funeral"
52.   A three-month maritime strike on the West Coast in
            1934 marked the determination of the workers to gain
            control of the hiring hall and terminate the abuse
            whereby the employers were able to decide at random
            who should and should not work, discriminate system-
            atically against those who tried to organize an effective
            union, and keep wages at a virtual starvation level.
            During the strike, the employers, city government, and
            police, with the full backing of the press and the

Chamber of Commerce, conducted a systematic reign of terror and vigilantism that culminated in the battle of Rincon Hill and the killing of Howard Sperry and Nick Bordoise by the San Francisco police. This event was followed by the General Strike, which paralyzed the city for three days.

Page 52.   "Thoor Ballylee"
Thoor Ballylee was the vacation home of William Butler Yeats. Pablo Neruda had a summer home on Isla Negra.

IN THE WINGS OF THE JUMP

Page 63.   "June 25, 1934 and Summer 1934."
See note for pp. 51–52 above.

Page 64.   Oleta O'Connor [Yates] subsequently became a Communist and was for many years an official of the Communist Party of San Francisco. Louis Goldblatt was subsequently Secretary-Treasurer of the International Longshoremen's and Warehousemen's Union for many years.

Edith A. Jenkins was born in San Francisco in 1913 and comes from a family of early German-Jewish settlers. From 1934 to 1956 she was involved variously in the student movement, the peace movement, women's peace organizations, and the Old Left. After taking a graduate degree in 1956, she taught English literature over the next twenty years, mainly at Merritt College in Oakland, and continued to be active in such causes as peace, the establishment of African-American and women's studies programs, and the teachers' union. She is married to David Jenkins, a labor activist and educator; they have four children and seven grandchildren.